FROM TURNBERRY TO TASMANIA

ADVENTURES OF A TRAVELING GOLFER

JOHN STEINBREDER

TAYLOR TRADE PUBLISHING
Lanham • Boulder • New York • London

Published by Taylor Trade Publishing
An imprint of The Rowman & Littlefield Publishing Group, Inc.
4501 Forbes Boulevard, Suite 200, Lanham, Maryland 20706
www.rowman.com

Unit A, Whitacre Mews, 26-34 Stannary Street, London SE11 4AB,
United Kingdom

Distributed by NATIONAL BOOK NETWORK

British Library Cataloguing in Publication Information Available

Library of Congress Cataloging-in-Publication Data Available
ISBN 978-1-58979-994-3 (cloth)
ISBN 978-1-58979-995-0 (electronic)

♾™ The paper used in this publication meets the minimum requirements of
American National Standard for Information Sciences—Permanence of Paper
for Printed Library Materials, ANSI/NISO Z39.48-1992.

Printed in the United States of America

To my mother, Cynthia Means Steinbreder,
who always encouraged me as a writer and endowed me
with a love of reading, traveling and learning.
God be with you until we meet again.

CONTENTS

THE NEW WORLD

INTRODUCTION

AMONG THE MOST SURPRISING AND SATISFYING ATTRI-
butes of golf is how well it lends itself to travel, and how it
gives practitioners the opportunity to play courses all over the
planet, see the world, and experience different people, places,
and things. It is a sport, to be sure, and serious good fun. But
golf is also a vehicle of discovery.

Start with the courses on which the game is played. Each
track is different in terms of design, locale, and look and can
be regarded as individual pieces of art. The best ones have
ways of truly testing the playing skills of golfers as they also
present them with the opportunities to hit shots that are both
pleasing and exciting, whether off elevated tees to ample landing areas or from closely cropped fairways to well-bunkered
greens. Great courses demand that players think their way
through their rounds and manage their games. And one cannot underestimate the joy that so many traveling golfers get

from experiencing the work of different designers and then analyzing their layouts after rounds, the way that art students might discuss the paintings they just viewed in a museum.

That sense of exploration and enlightenment gets particularly strong when a golfer tees it up on a historic course and considers the architect who laid out and built the track as well as the significant professional and amateur competitions it has hosted over the years. That's one of the things I fancy about a place such as the Lancashire coast in northwest England, and the opportunity to play hallowed retreats like Royal Liverpool, Royal Lytham & St. Annes, and Royal Birkdale, which have notable tournament histories, thanks to hosting numerous Open Championships, and also possess colorful and intriguing pasts as members clubs. At the same time, I find there is plenty to learn from and like about newer courses, such as Bandon Dunes and Old Macdonald in Oregon and Sand Hills in central Nebraska, for they offer keen insights on modern architecture and how designers today work with the land.

Then, there is the innate beauty of the vast majority of the tracks I have visited in my travels. As a rule, they are situated on attractive parcels of land. Along coasts, among piney woods, in nature preserves, and atop mountains. Just as appealing are the ways that golf courses can give a strong sense of the regions to which a player has traveled. Strolls around the Lost Farm course at Barnbougle in Tasmania that include encounters with tawny wallabies and blue-tongued lizards give players an unmistakable feel for the fauna of that faraway place, while the links of St. Andrews induce an instant and indelible sense of being on the Scottish coast, especially when the wind is blowing salty air across gnarly sand dunes and the steel-gray waters of the North Sea are roiling. And those sensations are only enhanced when those courses are walked, for walking allows you not only to see a place in a peaceful and unhurried way but also to absorb its many elements.

Some spots are so exotic and full of character that the education and enjoyment never stops, whether you are on the course or not. During one trip to Morocco, for example, I teed it up on one of King Hassan II's courses in the Imperial City of Meknes, a track laid out entirely inside the grounds of the royal palace. Afterward, I drove to the ancient Roman city of Volubilis, where I spent a couple of hours ambling down the stone streets of that historic site. Later that night, I dined on savory roasted lamb and sipped fragrant mint tea at a food stall in the Jemaa el Fna, or "Place of the Dead," next to the ancient souk in the heart of Marrakesh, still wearing my FootJoys and what turned out to be a daylong grin.

To be sure, treks to places previously unknown are a wanderer's delight. But golf as it exists for the traveling player rarely feels so foreign as to cause discomfort. For no matter how far afield the locations of the courses may be, no matter how wild and weird the settings, it is not hard to feel at home given the universality of the sport. Consider how many elements of a golf course and club are constants no matter where they are situated. Whether a welcoming pro shop or a proper locker room, a verdant putting green, or a spacious practice range. The first glimpses of the fairways and greens, the tees and bunkers of a golf course can make a player feel right at home, and so can a convivial 19th hole, where postround drinks are shared with newfound friends.

I also find that golf has a way of encouraging terrific camaraderie no matter what the locale. It enables people of all ages, abilities, and backgrounds to meld so easily. I have been in foursomes when the most common language is French or German, or one time even Arabic. Yet the group invariably came together as if it was composed of long lost friends, and no one was a stranger when our 18 holes were done.

The idea behind this book is to tell some of my stories from nearly two decades of traveling with my clubs and take readers to places they have never been as I also demonstrate how strong the connection between golf and travel is—and how it can lead them to embark on some very satisfying trips to all parts of the world.

The royal and ancient game has allowed me to wander like a modern-day Burton or Speke—from Turnberry to Tasmania and back again—and to experience not only the great golf courses but also the locales themselves, in all their splendor and beauty. It has been a terrific ride, and I hope that you as readers will enjoy it as well.

THE OLD WORLD

Greenland
(DENMARK)

Greenland
Sea

Jan Mayen
(NORWAY)

Barents
Sea

Denmark
Strait

Norwegian Sea

Hammerfest

Tromsø

Murmansk

Arctic Circle

Kiruna

White Sea

Arkhangel's

Reykjavik

ICELAND

North
Atlantic
Ocean

Luleå

Oulu

NORWAY

Umeå

FINLAND

SWEDEN

Lake
Ladoga

Trondheim

Tampere

Saint Petersburg

Tórshavn Faroe Islands
(DENMARK)

SHETLAND
ISLANDS

Bergen

Gulf
of
Bothnia

Turku Helsinki

Gävle

ÅLAND
ISLANDS

RUSSIA

Moscow

Rockall
(U.K.)

ORKNEY
ISLANDS

HEBRIDES

Stavanger

Oslo

Stockholm

Göteborg

Tallinn
ESTONIA

Gotland

Riga LATVIA

Smolensk

Aberdeen

North
Sea

DENMARK

Baltic Sea

LITHUANIA

Vitsyebsk

Glasgow
Edinburgh

UNITED

Malmö
Copenhagen

Öland

Vilnius

Mahilyow
Minsk

Belfast

Isle
of
Man
(U.K.)

Leeds

Bornholm

Kaliningrad

RUSSIA

BELARUS

Dublin

Irish
Sea

Manchester
Liverpool

Gdańsk

Hrodna

Homyel'

IRELAND

KINGDOM

Hamburg

Berlin

Poznań

Warsaw

Brest

Celtic
Sea

Cardiff

Birmingham

Amsterdam

NETH.

Bremen

POLAND

Łódź

Rivne

Kyiv

London

Rotterdam

Essen

Leipzig

Wrocław

UKRAINE

Guernsey (U.K.)
Jersey (U.K.)

English Channel

Brussels
Lille

BEL.

Cologne
Bonn

GERMANY

Frankfurt
am Main

Prague

Kraków

L'viv

Chernivtsi

Paris

LUX.

Luxembourg

CZECH REPUBLIC

Brno

SLOVAKIA

Mykolaji

Nantes

Strasbourg

Stuttgart

Munich

Bratislava

Cluj-
Napoca

Iaşi

Chisinau

MOLDOVA

Odes

Bay of
Biscay

FRANCE

Zürich
Bern
Geneva

LIECH.

Vaduz

Vienna

AUSTRIA

Budapest

ROMANIA

SWITZ.

Ljubljana

HUNGARY

Zagreb

Bucharest

Constanţa

MASSIF
CENTRAL

Lyon

Turin

Milan

Venice

SLOVENIA

Bordeaux

Genoa

CROATIA

BOSNIA AND
HERZEGOVINA

Belgrade

SERBIA

Varna

Blac
Sea

Bilbao

Toulouse

Florence

MONACO

SAN
MARINO

Sarajevo

Pristina

Sofia

BULGARIA

Istanbul

Porto

Zaragoza

Andorra
la Vella

ANDORRA

Marseille

ITALY

Rome

Adriatic
Sea

Podgorica

MONT.

Skopje

MACEDONIA

Thessaloníki

Bursa

PYRENEES

PORTUGAL

Madrid

Barcelona

Corsica

VATICAN
CITY

Naples

Tirana

ALB.

TURKE

Lisbon

SPAIN

Valencia

Balearic
Sea

Sardinia

Tyrrhenian
Sea

GREECE

İzmir

Sevilla

BALEARIC
ISLANDS

Cagliari

Athens

Gibraltar Málaga

Palermo

Ionian
Sea

Rhodes

Strait of Gibraltar

Ceuta
(SPAIN)

Alboran
Sea

Melilla
(SPAIN)

Oran

Algiers

Mediterranean Sea

Sicily

Aegean
Sea

Crete

Rabat

Casablanca

ALGERIA

Tunis

TUNISIA

Valletta

MALTA

Scale 1: 19,500,000

Lambert Conformal Conic Projection,
standard parallels 40°N and 56°N

300 Kilometers

0

0

300 Miles

1

ST. ANDREWS
At Home in the Home of Golf

As if the chance to play the Old Course isn't inducement enough to visit St. Andrews, as if the opportunity to tee it up on the other fine tracks on the links of the Auld Grey Toon isn't a good reason to fly right over, here's one more motive: there's no place on earth with so much good golf in such close proximity.

To be sure, everyone knows about the Old. If Scotland is golf's Holy Land, then the Old Course in St. Andrews is its Jerusalem. After all, it is where the royal and ancient game has been played since the fifteenth century, and where King James II banned the sport in 1457 because he believed it was distracting his soldiers from their archery practice. In addition, the Old has hosted twenty-nine British Open Championships as of this writing, far more than any other course. And most duffers are aware that there are other superb places to play on the links of St. Andrews. Like the New Course, a raw and rugged track that is actually more than a century old, and the Jubilee and Eden courses. But how many people truly comprehend all the amazing golfing riches that exist in and around this outpost in the Kingdom of Fife, courses of enormous strength and character that were formed centuries ago by some of the oldest golfing associations on earth?

I know I had never really contemplated that fact of golfing life in nearly two dozen trips to St. Andrews. But I got to thinking about all that is available during my latest pilgrimage to the town of sixteen thousand residents that is also famous for its fifteenth-century university as I nursed a smoky Oban in the Road Hole Bar in the Old Course Hotel. And I soon calculated that there are seventeen first-rate golf courses within an easy drive—or walk—of that very spot.

Start with the Old, where a round on this flattish, idiosyncratic layout with seven double greens is a truly religious experience. It is where golf history has long been made, and while some iconoclasts have gone so far as to suggest that the Old is not even worth playing, I believe that a round on that classic out-and-back track is about as good as it gets in golf. Especially when the wind is up and the gorse is in glorious bloom. And I do not know a finish quite so spectacular as that on the Old, playing into the ancient ecclesiastical center of St. Andrews with aged towers and spires rising from the huddle of its gray stone buildings.

Then, add in games on its neighbors, the New, the Jubilee, and the Eden as well as stylish Kingsbarns and the devilish Castle Course just out of town. Toss in the heathlands tracks called the Duke's up the hill as well as nasty Carnoustie nearly an hour's drive up the road, where Ben Hogan won the only Open Championship he ever entered, in 1953. A pair of lovely layouts awaits the player at Crail, and also those who tee it up at the Kittocks and the Torrance at St. Andrews Bay. And no one should overlook Ladybank and Scotscraig, or Lundin Links and Leven. Finally, there is Elie, whose most interesting feature is a large periscope mounted on the top of the starter's hut. It comes from a British submarine, the HMS *Excalibur,* and is used to see if the fairway on the first hole, which climbs up and over an imposing hill, is clear before the next group hits.

What an array of courses, I said to myself as I finished my whisky. And I was fairly staggered by the simple truth that had just come to me as I thought of playing all of those tracks over the years—and as I finally connected the dots for myself on what is perhaps the most pleasing picture a fanatic of the royal and ancient game can draw.

Great golf on seventeen great courses. All so close by, too, with my base the eminently charming burgh of St. Andrews, also home to the Royal and Ancient Golf Club, founded in 1754. I figure a player starting with a full tank of petrol in his rental car and a hefty supply of Advil in his golf bag could play 36 holes for eight days straight here and never have to travel more than sixty minutes at any given stretch. And he could probably count on getting on the Old at least once during his stay, whether through the ballot or by simply waiting by the starter's house for an open spot in a group.

I didn't have time to put that concept of a weeklong golf binge to the test on my most recent trip to St. Andrews. In fact, I only had a couple of days to play. But I managed to arrange an abbreviated version of what could serve as an enviable template for a longer stay.

I began one morning with an 8 a.m. tee time at Ladybank, one of the final qualifying courses for this year's Open Championship and an easy twenty minutes from the car park at the place where I usually hang my garment bag in St. Andrews, the Old Course Hotel. I ripped around the heathland gem, whose initial six holes were laid out by Old Tom Morris in 1879, in about three hours. After a quick lunch, I was off to another Open qualifier, Scotscraig. A sign by the pro shop says the club had formed in 1817 and described it as the thirteenth oldest golf association in the world. I teed it up with a pair of good-humored members, and the fast and firm fairways on this tight track occasionally pitched and rolled with wild undulations. My playing partners asserted that theirs was a second-shot course, and I quickly learned that analysis was correct. Unfortunately, the one thing I could not do that afternoon was hit a decent approach.

I was back in St. Andrews well before dusk that late spring evening, and felt not at all the worse for wear when I set off for the Crail Golfing Society the next morning. Neither the twisting road out of town nor the near-death experience of avoiding a suicidal cock pheasant that tried to cross in front of my rather fast-moving automobile, a flash of multihued feathers that brushed up and over my windshield, slowed my travel time to that lyrically named retreat. In fact, I made it there in roughly twenty minutes, and then happily scooted around the so-called Balcomie Links in equally efficient fashion. Between shots on the coastal course, which was also designed by Old Tom Morris, my playing partner provided interesting bits of club history, my favorite of which was about the first Captain of Crail, William Ranken, who fought for the British army during the American Revolutionary War a few years before the club's founding in 1786. The deft routing was something to behold, and so was the scenery, whether of the seals that bobbed in the North Sea, the fishing boats that chugged up and down the rocky shore, or the flocks of eiders that skirted the tops of the whitecaps as they flew from cove to cove.

My final stop this day, and on this all-too-short trip, was Lundin Links. Founded in 1868, it was yet another enticing seaside track with testy breezes and devilish bunker complexes. My game faltered badly on the back nine, but I was still able to discern what a great test of golf this was and what great fun Lundin Links was to play.

I easily could do this for a full week, I thought to myself as I enjoyed a speedy, pheasant-free ride back to the Old Course Hotel, past fields of barley, berries, and potatoes and by hillsides yellow with rapeseed. In fact, I envisioned myself enjoying a succession of days like that, a golfer's version of *Groundhog Day* with each one starting and ending the same way—but with the hours in between filled with rounds on courses located in and around this lovely town. I begin my mornings in the Old Course Hotel, just as the sun is rising above the North Sea (and without "I Got You, Babe" playing on the radio). I drink coffee for a spell and look at the maintenance crew getting the Old, New, and Jube ready for the day. Later, I watch the first players of the morning step onto the first tee of the Old. I cannot see them clearly, or hear a thing they say. But I feel their excitement, the excitement any golfer feels when he steps onto that special spot. And that gets me juiced about the places I am about to play.

Whatever those courses may be on this particular day, I know they are all fine tracks—and know that I am not going to have to travel very far to enjoy them. I get in my first 18, enjoy a chilly Bellhaven with my playing partners afterward, and then finish my second round. It's only 6 p.m. and still light out when I return to the hotel. If I am feeling somewhat prosperous, I enjoy a massage in the Kohler Water Spa, which is located in the Old Course Hotel. If not, I repair to the superb tubs and showers Herb Kohler put in when he bought this historic inn in 2004. The high-pressure bursts of water they produce can revive even the most battered golfing body.

And I want to be revived because I want to see my friends Jack and Sheena Willoughby at the Dunvegan Hotel, situated just behind the 18th green of the Old. The bar there is the best 19th hole in the game, a beguiling retreat where the beer is cold, the company convivial and all about golf, the service first rate, and the food as satisfying as the courses we have been playing that day. I throw down another Bellhaven, order the Dunvegan steak medium, and enjoy a glass of claret when the piece of tasty Aberdeen beef is plopped down at my place at the bar. It's hauntingly quiet as I stroll back to my hotel, down the dark street that runs past the Valley of Sin and the Swilcan Bridge, the Road Hole bunker, and the old railway stationmaster's house that is now the Jigger Inn.

I am tired when I climb into bed, but am ready to do it all over again. I am in *Groundhog Day*, only with golf clubs, and I love every minute of it.

Even if Andie MacDowell is nowhere to be found.

2

NORTHWEST IRELAND
Return of the Quiet Man

IT'S LASHING RAIN AS I PREPARE TO HIT MY DRIVE ON THE 15th hole of the Narin & Portnoo Golf Club. Windy and cold, too. But I could not be happier. Part of it is the seaside setting, standing as I am on a tee cut amid grassy dunes and along a beach curved in the shape of a crescent moon. I also like that this is the third par-five I have played in a row, on a track first laid out in 1930 by residents of this quiet burg and subsequently revamped over the years. I give them credit for working with what the scruffy linksland gave them and not trying to force a more conventional design.

The number of hares scurrying across the grounds reminds me that this once was a rabbit warren—and tell me that golf has done little to infringe upon their habitat. And I chuckle as I hear the "baas" of sheep grazing in the leas to the east. Those sounds speak to the agricultural character of this part of the world and how much farming remains a way of life.

I also marvel at the hills that stretch out beyond the livestock, some sections brilliant yellow, thanks to the flowering gorse, and others copper in color, from the swathes of heather still weeks away from blooming. Neat, moss-covered stonewalls and gnarly hedgerows run through the lush land, dividing it into fields, and a chilly fog shrouds the highest points.

But what really has me grinning, even though my round up to this point has felt like one long walk through a car wash, is the sensation of how the northwest is Ireland at its very best. With simple links and modest clubhouses. With the whitewashed homes that make up the sleepy fishing villages and farming towns, and the warm pubs and cozy restaurants where drinks and dinners are shared after games. With tidy country lanes where road signs are in both English and Gaelic. The quiet pace of life in this region and low cost of living add to the enviable atmosphere, as do the people, so "nice and handy" as they say in these parts. Especially the men and women who play the game—and belong to the clubs—not because those actions fulfill some social agenda but because they love golf.

These things combine to make this area the Ireland first-time visitors expect to find when they venture here, and the country returning travelers hope to see every time they come back. It is the land of *The Quiet Man* and a locale whose ethos harkens back to easier, less hectic times.

It is also one hell of a place to tee it up.

Even in the biting rain, Narin & Portnoo ranks among my favorites anywhere. That's largely because it is a true links, playing firm and fast, with undulating fairways that frequently send tee shots bouncing in all directions and so often leave golfers with uneven lies. I also like that a number of its holes play along the water. Like No. 15, which this day is so buffeted by wind that I have to start my drive over the edge of the beach so it has a chance of settling on the fairway. Then, there is the 8th, a short par-four that plays to a small green set on a tiny promontory jutting into the ocean. Almost as good is the uphill drive off No. 9, from a tee built on that same sliver of land. Seagulls hover nearby in the wind as I tee off, squawking as they scour the rocks for something to eat.

Equally as fun is the nearby Donegal Golf Club, also known as Murvagh, a rugged Eddie Hackett creation with some architectural assistance from noted golf writer and course designer Pat Ruddy. Laid out on a small peninsula with brilliantly designed green complexes, it demands precise approaches. I enjoy the oyster beds I see in the estuary off the 4th hole and let my mind wander to what I hope to be having for dinner. I also relish the hybrid I have to hit into a strong wind over the so-called Valley of Tears on the par-three 5th and get a kick out of the story my host tells me of how members at this modest retreat, in typical community fashion, get together once a week to fill in divots on the fairways. He then informs me that Darren Clarke, winner of the 2011 British Open Championship, describes the sweeping links of Murvagh as one of his favorites. After just one round, I can well see why.

At the very top of Ireland is the Rosapenna resort, with two exceptional tracks in the town of Downings along Sheephaven Bay. One was built in the 1890s by the old master, Old Tom Morris, and revamped in later years by the equally extolled Harry Vardon and James Braid. And the other was designed more than a century later by Ruddy, who also laid out the awesome European Club south of Dublin. Old Tom kept to the flattish lowlands by the water when he made his course at Rosapenna, largely because it was not so easy to move earth in his day. But Ruddy laid out his track, dubbed Sandy Hills, in the dunes above Old Tom's, and he produced a course both beautiful and beguiling, with stunning tee shots, devilish pot bunkers, and deftly crafted greens that are as fair as they are fun. It can play big, at more than 7,200 yards from the tips, but I was quite pleased to see it from a much more sensible 6,400 yards, which is where the white markers measure out.

To the southwest of that retreat is County Sligo, also known as Rosses Point, a superb seaside links crafted by the great Harry Colt in the shadow of the flat-topped, limestone mountain known as Ben Bulben. The first four holes run up and around a massive dune, and then comes the par-five 5th, known appropriately as the Jump, where drives are hit from high atop a cliff to a fairway far below. The last six holes of this gem run along the water, and I am inspired by the visuals of those holes, and also by the knowledge that the poet W. B. Yeats often wrote about this part of the northwest, for it was the place from which his parents hailed—and where he spent a great deal of time as a child. His poem "Under Ben Bulben" is well worth a postround read.

Not surprisingly, I fall hard for Enniscrone as well. The first green of this Eddie Hackett/Donald Steel design is tucked in the dunes, and there is a lot to commend all that follows, especially on the back nine. The short par-fours at Nos. 12 and 13 are a joy, and the stretch of 14, 15, and 16, two par-fives bookending a meaty par-four along the Atlantic as waves crash onto the beach and wind rumbles, is as good a trio of holes as exists in the British Isles. As is the case with most courses in the northwest, there are not many bunkers at Enniscrone. But that doesn't mean there is anything easy about golf in this region, for the wind and the gnarly marram grass quite ably protect par.

Then, there is Carne, which Hackett routed through dunes that rise in some cases two hundred feet high. To get to that course, I have to drive by the Ceide Fields, a Neolithic site that contains the oldest known stonewalled fields in the world, dating back nearly six thousand years. And even though I am anxious to get to Carne, I stop for a quick walk around those ruins, happily surprised to find such history in the midst of golf country.

It was a very worthwhile respite, and I relished the round that followed just as much. The rugged topography of Carne makes for some very dramatic tee shots, especially off No. 18, where drives are hit from the highest point on the property and golfers can take in views of the nearby waters of Blacksod Bay and the Nephin Mountain range. The track also lends itself to some thrilling approaches into greens tucked among grassy knolls. It is golf in its most compelling state, and also its most aerobic, especially if you are carrying your own bag.

I like Carne for all those reasons. And the rest of the golf courses I played in the northwest, too. It's the Ireland we as golfers have always expected and hoped it would be.

It is also the best place to savor the work of Ireland's most noteworthy architect, Eddie Hackett. His name is not as renowned as Donald Ross. Nor is his work nearly as celebrated as that of Alister MacKenzie or Charles Blair Macdonald. But when you play golf in the northwest of Ireland, the course architect you hear most about is Eddie Hackett. And understandably so, because he designed or revamped many of the best links layouts in that region, such as Carne, Enniscrone, Connemara, Ballyliffin, and Murvagh.

Born in Dublin in 1910, Hackett suffered from tuberculosis as a young boy, which kept him from being able to play active sports. So he took to teeing it up with his father. As a teenager, Hackett went to work at the Royal Dublin Golf Club and got good enough to become head professional at Royal Portmarnock—and to compete in a handful of British Open Championships. Later on, he took to designing golf courses, and when it came to his approach to architecture, he often said: "I find nature is the best architect, and I simply try to dress up what the Good Lord provides."

Carne is one of Hackett's greatest creations, so pleasingly natural and extraordinarily beautiful. One of the club directors, Eamon Mangan, has nothing but fond memories of working with the Dublin designer. "Eddie was such a gentleman, a first-class saint," he recalls. "He was seventy-six years old when he came to work here, and went to mass daily. He wanted the wind and the elements to shape things. He didn't like bulldozers, and he always insisted on walking the land, not walking over it, so he could feel the ground with which he was working."

Now the general manager of North & West Coast Links, John McLaughlin remembers Hackett from the days when McLaughlin worked at Connemara Golf Links in western Ireland—and when Hackett was working on that course. "The first thing I recall is the way he was with his fee," McLaughlin says. "He told the club to pay him what it could when it could. He was that way all the time. Whatever the course or clubs could afford, he would take. He was a slight man who could walk the hills but had a hard time getting over the fences. So Eddie would lie on the ground, I would lift up the bottom of the fence, and he would roll underneath it. He loved golf course architecture, and he loved the northwest of Ireland."

As do so many others.

3

ENGLAND'S LANCASHIRE COAST

Museum Pieces

I'M A HISTORY BUFF, WHICH MEANS I TRY TO DEVOTE prodigious portions of my travel time visiting ruins and museums. Even on golf trips I almost always balance the hours I spend on courses with stops at local places of interest, to feed my cultural appetite as much as the one I have for the royal and ancient game.

I say almost because I didn't make any off-course plans when I recently visited England's Lancashire Coast. There were no afternoons at the celebrated branch of the Tate Museum in Liverpool, nor tours dedicated to the legacy of its hometown band, the Beatles, and other prominent pop music groups that sprung from its gritty streets in the 1960s. Forget walks down Penny Lane or ferries across the Mersey. It was golf this time around, and golf only.

But golf from a very strong historical perspective given the courses I was playing, ones that more than satisfied my need for intellectual enrichment. For each of the places I visited was a museum unto itself. Like Royal Liverpool, host of twelve British Opens and eighteen British Amateurs since its founding in 1869. Or Royal Birkdale, where nine Opens have been contested, and where Arnold Palmer, Lee Trevino, Johnny Miller, and Tom Watson all hoisted Claret Jugs. Birkdale is also the site of two Ryder Cups, and the one in which Jack Nicklaus famously conceded Tony Jacklin's putt. Then there is Royal Lytham St. Anne's, which has held eleven Open Championships as well as a pair of Ryder Cups. Bobby Jones made his miracle bunker shot on the 17th there that all but secured his win at the 1926 Open. And it's the course on which the late, great Seve Ballesteros hit an otherworldly wedge from the makeshift car park on No. 16 within fifteen feet of the cup on the way to his first Open Championship victory in 1979—and then made the birdie putt.

Those Lancashire courses are so historically rich they even have plaques in the ground honoring some of those great shots. Such as the one on the right side of the 16th fairway at Birkdale, the spot from which Palmer muscled his approach from the gorse onto the green during the last round of the 1961 Open he won. In addition, their stately clubhouses boast expansive exhibits of clubs, golf balls, scorecards, and other memorabilia that not only recount the championships they hosted and the players who won them but also tell some of the best stories the game has ever spawned.

In writing about the links of Hoylake, Bernard Darwin opined that while it belonged to the members of Royal Liverpool, it also was a part of "the whole world of golf, for it has played a great part in the history of the game." Truer words have rarely been scribed, but Darwin might as well have been talking about Birkdale and Lytham, too. Or Formby Golf Club, the fourth course I played on my tour of this region and the site of four British Amateurs, including the

1984 championship that saw José María Olazábal beat Colin Montgomerie in the finals. They are great monuments of a great game, yet remain highly relevant as they continue to host major championships in the modern era.

They are also a lot of fun to play.

Lytham is a flattish track and tight off the tees, a thinking man's course pocked with more than two hundred pot bunkers that quite ably protect par. The Irish Sea is nearby but never in view. Suburban homes surround the track and a commuter train line runs along the south side of the layout, which was revamped by Harry Colt just before World War I. Darwin once described Lytham as a "just beast," and he must have come to that characterization after playing it on a day when the wind was blowing, for it can surely howl there.

I spent a night in the delightfully spartan Dormy House at Lytham, and woke just after dawn the following day to the sound of mowers humming across the grass on the practice putting green just below my bedroom window. The sun was bathing that section of grass with soft light, along with the first hole that stretched out before me. It was a par-three, playing some 225 yards from the tips, and I suddenly remembered that Lytham is the only course in the British Open Championship Rota that starts with a three-par. I was first off the tee that morning, and I ripped around in just over a couple of hours, lugging my bag and managing to avoid all but a couple of the deep pot bunkers that make scoring so difficult there. I savored the sound of the commuter train that runs by the southern border of the course, happily considering how many good golf courses are located near railroad lines. As I approached the 18th green, I could not help but think of Gary Player overcooking his approach the year he won his Open here, in 1974—his golf ball coming to rest next to the red brick clubhouse. He had to putt left-handed to get his third shot onto the green. It was also hard not to consider all the great golfers who have claimed Open championships on that course. Jones, Jacklin, and Ballesteros. Peter Thomson, Bob Charles, and Bobby Locke, as well as Tom Lehman and David Duval. And Ernie Els in 2012, after Adam Scott demonstrated how hard it can be to close in a major championship when he bogeyed the last four holes to finish one back of the South African.

After my round, I wandered through Lytham's clubhouse, examining the check Jacklin received for taking the 1969 Open title there, all 4,250 pounds sterling of it. There is Bobby Jones's scorecard from the 1926 Championship, and Seve's nine iron from his win in 1979. One of the club workers sidled up to tell me the story of Lehman making a promise the night before he played his final round in the 1996 Open Championship—and the day after he shot a blistering 64—to buy the entire staff a drink if he won. And there he was at 10:30 that Sunday night, keeping his word, Claret Jug in hand.

Royal Birkdale is routed in and among the dunes outside of Southport, with gaping pot bunkers and ample greens that break ever so subtly. The wind can blow there as well, right off the Irish Sea that first comes into view on No. 6. Though there are more changes of elevation than at Lytham, the fairways at Birkdale are fairly flat, as are the lies off of them. Swathes of gorse create good cover for the regal ring-necked pheasants that occasionally strut across the grounds—and create misery for golfers who dump shots into them. Though it hosted its first Open in 1954, Birkdale has been a regular part of the Rota ever since, most recently in 2008, when Padraig Harrington came out on top. Its formidable roster of Open winners attests to the very high quality of the golf course, and so does the way Birkdale finishes, with three par-fives in the last four holes (for mere mortal golfers, that is, as the pros play 18 as a par-four).

Fair Formby is a gem, too. Less well known than the three Open venues in Lancashire, to be sure, but it is just as compelling a golf experience. Though most definitely a links, Formby features stands of pines that also give it a parklands feel, and a number of the holes boast elevated tees that make the mere act of driving a ball down the middle of the fairway as pleasurable a moment as there is in golf. Especially on Nos. 8 and 9. The Irish Sea is visible for the first time off of the tee of the par-three 10th, and a number of holes run among grassy dunes in that portion of the course. Matteo Manassero won the 2009 British Amateur at Formby, and I do not know of a better place in Great Britain to lounge after a game than the room on the second floor of the magnificent clubhouse, gazing out windows that provide sweeping views of the verdant course. Club member Paul Jenkins showed me another postround option when he took me on a golf cart ride out to a bench by the 11th hole. He had strapped a cooler to the back of that vehicle and from it extracted a chilled bottle of Sancerre, two dozen oysters, a corkscrew, and a shucking knife. We sat quietly at that spot for the next hour, gazing across grassy dunes to the Irish Sea beyond, washing down those luscious mollusks with crisp white wine.

Finally, there is hallowed Hoylake, which is what Royal Liverpool is often called because that's the name of the village in which it is located. Hoylake is where Walter Hagen and Jones won Open championships, and Thomson, Roberto De Vicenzo, and Tiger Woods, too. Built on what then was the race course of the Liverpool Hunt Club, it is a classic links flanked on the west side by the River Dee, with much of the flatness of Lytham and a bit of the dunes found at Formby and Birkdale. Holes 9, 10, 11, and 12 run along the Dee, and Hoylake is one of those places where the wind must blow to keep the great golfers honest. Tiger famously kept the driver in his bag for most of the 2006 Open Championship, playing his two iron off the tee with great precision time and time again. That very club is displayed in the splendid Royal Liverpool clubhouse, as is a silver bowl Young Tom Morris won in an 1872 tournament there. It's the past and present of golf all in one place, and that fact is driven home even harder by the thought that Royal Liverpool hosted the first British Amateur ever played, in 1885, and was the venue of the Open Championship once again in 2014.

That's the beauty of these places. Museum pieces one and all, yet still very much alive. They remain destinations for the best pros and amateurs, and for the recreational golfer looking for a big taste of golf history as he plays some of the best courses in the game.

4

DUBLIN
Links Golf and Literature

WHILE THERE IS MUCH TO COMMEND THIS CITY ON THE River Liffey, two things stand above all others—links golf and literature. Some of the finest layouts in the world are within easy driving distance of Dublin: Royal Portmarnock and Island Golf Club, to name a pair, and they merit acclaim for the character of their green complexes as well as the ways they snake around wind-whipped dunes. County Louth and Royal Dublin get high marks for the shot making they demand, and the scenic masterpiece Pat Ruddy crafted at the European Club deserves to be ranked among the best modern links courses in the world, especially when golfers consider how brilliantly it sets up off the tees.

As for literature, Dublin has long been to writing what Florence has been to art, a place where the very best in the business lived, worked, and played. Three Dubliners have won Nobel Prizes for Literature—William Butler Yeats, George

Bernard Shaw, and Samuel Beckett. The city is also where James Joyce set *Ulysses* and where Oscar Wilde and Bram Stoker went to school (at Trinity College). Jonathan Swift was born in Dublin and is buried there. Men like these wrote their most profound words here and found inspiration for the characters they immortalized in their creations.

A number of its writers made their marks in Dublin as characters themselves. Shaw may have been a teetotaler, and Beckett not much of a boozer. But many of the city's best scribes also happened to be scratch drinkers and were often found in watering holes such as Davy Byrne's and McDaid's. The connection between pub and poet in Dublin is huge, and perhaps no one personified that better than the dramatist Brendan Behan, who beveraged himself to an early death in the early 1960s but not before he declared: "I am not a writer with a drinking problem, but rather a drinker with a writing problem."

Dubliners like their literature, and they fancy their golf, too. And that's why my goal during my last visit there was to get to know its golf, and writers, better. My plan was simple: tee it up in the mornings, and then turn to literature for the rest of the day, whether rereading, say, *Ulysses* or touring the museums and libraries that celebrate the lives and works of Dublin's scribes.

I began my trip with a round at the closest course to downtown, Royal Dublin. Founded in 1885, the track was built on a 600-acre spit of land formed in the early nineteenth century when Captain Bligh of *Mutiny on the Bounty* fame constructed a huge seawall from the shore into Dublin Bay, turning a series of semisubmerged sand bars into what came to be called Bull Island. The par-72 track routed there is one of Ireland's best, a classic out-and-back with firm and fast fairways, subtle yet strategic bunkers, and greens that are very receptive to run-up shots, even when the wind is howling.

Good as that track is, however, nearby Royal Portmarnock is even better. The opening hole is set hard by an estuary and backs up to a small pro shop, giving golfers an instant feel for what lays ahead—a lovely links with rugged dunes, gnarly bunkering, and occasional water views. The long, par-four 4th that runs along the sea is a delight when it plays downwind, requiring a big drive with a slight draw to a dune-lined fairway with a series of bunkers running down the right side, and then a precise approach shot to a large green. I immediately decided that is my favorite hole, but quickly changed my mind after playing the par-five 6th, and then the three-par 7th. On my way in, I made par on 14, which Henry Cotton once described as his favorite hole. Then I snagged another on the par-three 15th, the one Ben Crenshaw said was the shortest *par-five* in golf. And when I putted out on 18, I realized Bernard Darwin might have gotten it right when he wrote that the last five holes at Royal Portmarnock are the best finishing holes in golf. By the end of the round, I have determined that I like each and every hole there, which helps explain why Royal Portmarnock has had twenty Irish Opens since its founding in 1894, as well as one British Amateur (in 1949) and the 1991 Walker Cup.

True to design, I followed my round at Royal Dublin with a visit to the Dublin Writer's Museum, which is housed in a restored eighteenth-century mansion once owned by the Jameson family of whisky-making fame. I happily spent about an hour wandering through its collection, which spans three centuries of books, letters, and personal items belonging to Joyce and Beckett as well as Swift and Shaw. The next day, when my golf at Portmarnock was done, I wandered around the Long Room at the Old Library at Trinity College, which Queen Elizabeth I founded in 1592. Measuring some seventy yards in length, it boasts roughly two hundred thousand of the library's oldest books. Trinity also houses the stunning

Book of Kells, an extremely rare, lavishly illustrated rendering of the four gospels written in Latin by monks around 800 AD, and I made sure to check that out as well.

Of course, man cannot live by books alone. Especially a man with golf clubs in tow. So it was back to the links the next morning. This time, my game was set for the Island Golf Club just outside the north Dublin village of Malahide. While the retreat does not have as impressive a history of championships as Portmarnock, its links layout deserves to be mentioned with the great layouts of this land. Holes are routed among shaggy, rolling dunes, and the arbitrary undulations of the fairways and greens test both patience and skill. Accuracy is key, and so is distance control. Yet for as testing as the Island can be, I couldn't keep myself from smiling during my round, even after enduring bad bounces and more than a few bad swings. The shots I had to make, from the tees, off the fairways, and over and around the pot bunkers, were simply that much fun, especially with the wind blowing fifteen knots.

Several miles north of the Island is County Louth. Located in the small fishing village of Baltry, it, too, is an oldie, having been formed in 1892. And it has also held its fair share of golf championships, among them the 1950 Irish Amateur and the 2009 Irish Open. The pleasure in playing a round there is the austerity of the layout, and the natural way that architect Donald Steel enhanced the course Tom Simpson revamped just before World War II. The back-to-back par-fives at Nos. 2 and 3 speak to a designer's desire to work with what the land gave him, and the appearance of another five-par at the 6th drives that fact home. The highlight may well be the 14th tee, which is built atop a massive sand dune and provides a sweeping view of County Louth as well as an enticing spot from which to hit a drive on this short (332 yards) par-four. It also is the place from which I watched the greenskeeper release a brace of dogs trained to track down the rabbits that dig holes throughout the links. The dogs quickly disappeared into the dunes, and a few minutes later I heard some rather excited yelps, which told me the hounds had successfully reduced the cottontail population at County Louth by at least one.

The last course I sampled was the European Club, located about an hour's drive south of the city. A modern links that opened in 1992, it was built and designed by the noted golf writer and raconteur Pat Ruddy and quickly soared to the top of most golfers' must-play lists. The sandy soil on which the course is constructed drains perfectly, the fairways run with requisite speed and unpredictability, and the bunkering is fiendish yet fair. As for the individual holes, Nos. 12 and 13 may be two of the most scenic and enjoyable I have ever played, running along the Irish Sea and demanding that players be both long and accurate. But my favorites may well be the two extra holes Ruddy added to make the European Club a 20-hole layout, the par-threes known as 7a and 12a. They are novelties, in a sense, and only enhance the sense of pleasure one already gets from playing there.

Pleasure came in another form when I returned to Dublin that afternoon for another literary interlude. I thought about visiting the James Joyce Museum, or possibly the Abbey Theatre, which was cofounded by William Butler Yeats nearly a century ago and regularly stages plays by some of Ireland's best writers, past and present. I even considered touring the place where George Bernard Shaw was born and seeing Jonathan Swift's tombstone in St. Patrick Cathedral. But in the end, I decided to amble over to the Duke Pub at cocktail hour for the beginning of an acclaimed literary pub crawl through several of Dublin's finest pubs, all of which have literary connections. The tour took a couple of hours, and I quaffed pints with newfound friends as we listened to

a pair of actors recite the words of Shaw, Swift, and Wilde—
and tell stories about their life and times in Dublin. We
ended the evening in Davy Byrne's, the pub where Leopold
Bloom, Joyce's memorable character from *Ulysses*, ordered his
Gorgonzola cheese sandwich and glass of Burgundy. Beckett
drank there as well, in the 1930s, and scribes like Behan and
the "peasant poet" Patrick Kavanagh emptied more than a
few glasses there years later.

So I decided to savor a Guinness in Davy Byrne's, too, in
honor of Dublin's great writers as well as its great golf, bringing a fitting end to a trip involving the two best things the city
has to offer.

5

SCOTLAND
North by Northeast

WHEN IT COMES TO PICKING VENUES FOR ITS TOURNA-
ments, the R&A knows what it's doing. Not only for its
flagship event, the Open Championship, but also for its
other competitions, such as the Walker Cup and the British
Amateur. To be sure, the organization always goes for great
golf courses. But the quality of the layout is the only real con-
sideration when it considers its less prominent contests, as
the R&A doesn't have to worry in those cases about having
enough hotel rooms, for example, or space for parking and
hospitality. The choice is purer, as a result, because the crite-
rion is all about the golf.

That's why discerning golfers seek out the courses and
clubs that host those sorts of events. They know the spots are
among the finest in the British Isles. And they understand that
one of the best places to find them is in the north and northeast of Scotland.

Royal Aberdeen is there, host of the 2011 Walker Cup and the site of the 2005 Senior Open Championship, won by Tom Watson. So is Royal Dornoch, venue of the 1985 Amateur. Another must-play is Nairn, where Colin Montgomerie (Monty) captured the Amateur Championship in 1994, where the Walker Cup was contested in 1999 and the Curtis Cup in 2012. And while the R&A had nothing to do with bringing the Scottish Open to Castle Stuart for three years, 2011 to 2013, the fact that the European PGA Tour thought it good enough to host one of its tournaments speaks to how good that layout really is.

Of course, there are other superb courses in this part of the world that haven't had the privilege of holding significant championships even though they are more than worthy. Like Cruden Bay, a stunning seaside links designed in part by Old Tom Morris, and Murcar, which abuts Royal Aberdeen. There is also Moray, just down the road from Nairn, where US Walker Cup team captain Jim Holtgrieve brought his charges to practices before the 2011 matches. The spectacular track that Donald Trump asked Martin Hawtree to construct for him in Aberdeen has yet to host any tournaments of note, but that is only because it is such a newcomer, having only opened in 2012. Golfers can be sure that, given the very high quality of its design and setting, it will certainly be the site of many significant competitions down the road.

Then there is Askernish, the Ghost Course on the Hebridean isle of South Uist off Scotland's northwest coast, built by Old Tom Morris in the late 1880s and abandoned for nearly a century before locals recovered the marvelous seaside track and began playing golf there again.

That's quite a collection, and what makes it even better is that they are all links courses—and all part of a golfing frontier well worth exploring. They do lie well north of popular golf destinations around Glasgow and St. Andrews, but the traveler who endures the extra travel time to play these layouts is richly rewarded.

The Balgownie Links of Royal Aberdeen is a good place to start. The tee of the opening hole backs up to the clubhouse, and the North Sea spreads out beyond the first green. The course then turns hard left after the straightforward four-par, and Nos. 2–9 run along the water. The bunkering is tough, yet restrained, and the tight, undulating fairways and devilish greens snake in and around the dunes.

The back nine smartly works it way back to the clubhouse, through somewhat less dramatic land set a bit farther back from the water across which tankers carry oil to and from the petroleum center of the British Isles. The views across the course to the sea never disappoint, and neither do the challenges of the varied shots that must be hit on each hole. And as the American Walker Cuppers discovered to their collective dismay during their loss to the team from Great Britain and Ireland in the 2011 matches there, the wind can really howl.

A wee drive up the coast is Cruden Bay, and it awes players right away with a distant view off the first tee of Slains Castle, which served as a model for Bram Stoker when he wrote *Dracula* in this burg. The front nine wind through towering dunes and offer challenges both long and short. Like the par-four 3rd, which measures only 274 yards from the tips but plays as tough as a hole twice that length, with out-of-bounds down the left side and behind the green, devious mounding on the right, and a slick putting surface loathe to hold anything but the most perfect shot. I played driver here, with a draw that took advantage of a hard right-to-left wind. Then, on No. 4, a par-three nearly 200 yards directly into that near gale, I hit driver again, only this time with a slight cut. I felt a great sense of relief when I managed my second par in a row. But I quickly realized I had a lot more work to do when I hiked to the top of the dune on which the tee of the par-four 5th is laid out—and contemplated that 455-yard monster.

As for the back at Cruden Bay, it has its share of good holes, too. Especially Nos. 12 and 13, where a twisting burn comes into play, and also the par-four 14th, which runs along the North Sea and requires a blind approach to a funky green, tucked in the dunes and as narrow as it is long.

I could not help but ponder what a classic links Cruden Bay is as I walked to the 15th tee there. And I started ticking off in my head the many things I like about these types of courses. I enjoy how they force you to adjust your swing from shot to shot, depending upon the wind and the ways the holes are routed. I love when I have to move from punching low shots to lofting high balls, from swinging free and easy downwind to be a bit tighter when going into a gale. I also delight in how I have to think harder on a links because there are so many nuances to each play, and to remember to take what the course gives me, shrugging off the bad bounces and bum luck that are so much a part of this game.

It is tortuous at times, but also titillating, and I decide that much of the pleasure I derive from links golf stems from the way it compels me to play the game in its most basic form, and to experience courses built by the Old Masters in the ways they had to play them, too. Such as Cruden, which was also designed in part by Old Tom Morris. It's a way of stepping back in time and paying homage to the pioneers of the game, as it is also a mode of getting to know this historic land better.

Nairn is another classic course. Located due west of Cruden Bay and laid out on the Moray Firth outside Inverness, it is a flattish links with an impressive architectural pedigree, having been worked at different times by Old Tom and five-time Open champion James Braid. Nairn is also as strong a championship venue as it is a pleasing place for members to play every day. Local golfers heartily sing its praises, and Monty likes it so much that he named a house of his after it.

The opening seven holes run right along the Firth, and the first thing a golfer realizes is that this course is a lot about the bunkering. Drives must be accurate to stay out of those strategically placed fairway hazards, and greenside bunkers must be avoided on approaches. Alas, there is not much in the way of reprieves for those who get onto the putting surfaces at Nairn, for their testy undulations give even the best golfers fits. I fell especially hard for the par-threes there, among them the shortish 4th, which plays to a well-bunkered, kidney-shaped green, and the downhill 14th, some 220 yards from the tips to a putting surface guarded by four bunkers in front and a mess of gorse left and back.

A few miles down the road from Nairn is the new kid on the block, Castle Stuart. Built by Mark Parsinen, who created the superb Kingsbarn course outside St. Andrews, and opened in 2009, it is a modern links of great style and substance, not as flat as Nairn yet not as dunesy as Aberdeen or Cruden Bay. Parsinen shares design credit here with American architect Gil Hanse, and they offer a beguiling mix of holes that are routed through swathes of gorse and broom as well as heather and sea marram. The fairways are wide, and the greens generous. But errant shots quite easily find trouble. Several holes run along the Moray Firth, and the water is almost always in view. Not surprisingly, the panoramas are pretty special, too. Like the ones behind the 305-yard par-four 3rd, which boasts what might be best described as an "infinity" green and makes the short approach feel a bit like the tee shot on No. 7 at Pebble Beach. Or the sight of the Chanonry Lighthouse behind Nos. 10 and 11. And players will occasionally catch glimpses of the actual Castle Stuart, which was built in 1625 by James Stuart, the 3rd Earl of Moray, and restored in the late 1970s by his descendants, who now operate it as a small inn.

About an hour up the road from there is Royal Dornoch. With its routing over two distinct levels of dunes and views of the sea from every hole. With its exceptional Old Tom Morris design that has induced golfers as wide ranging as Tom Watson and Harry Vardon to gush after playing rounds there. With its history as the home of the fabled architect Donald Ross, who also served as the club's golf professional and greenskeeper (and who did a brilliant job of revamping the first two holes). With its location in a sleepy Scottish town of twelve hundred people that lolls happily through life. Ross's brother Alec, who won the 1907 US Open, played out of Dornoch, and so did industrialist Andrew Carnegie, who lived nearby in Skibo Castle and served as club VP for a spell. Like so many golfers before and after them, they became enthralled as much by the almost mystical ethos of a place so scenic and serene as they were by the golf, which ranks as good as any in the world.

Standing on the 5th tee at Royal Dornoch during my first round there, I swore I could hear the sweetly subdued strains of Mark Knopler's guitar as my ears also caught the sounds of waves breaking on the beach to my right. I stepped back to gaze across the distant water for a bit, seeing faint outlines of seals bobbing in the Firth. The song became a bit louder, and I was sure that as I listened to that tune, called "Going Home," and felt the sudden rumble of an RAF fighter jet roaring by, I had somehow walked right into *Local Hero*.

To me, *Local Hero* is a damn near perfect movie. A Texas oilman named Mac travels to a coastal Scottish village to buy up the town so his company can build a refinery there, but he becomes so enchanted with the place that he doesn't want to do anything to spoil it. Nor does he want to leave. It is a movie of charm and wit, featuring the sorts of seals that ancient mariners once thought were mermaids, and a real mermaid named Marina who tries to set that record straight.

It even has fighter jets that serve as a reminder of how badly human encroachment can spoil even the most beautiful settings. And it speaks quite eloquently to the possibilities of finding utter perfection in life and the understandable desires of never wanting to leave places that have it.

I quickly determined during that maiden round that Dornoch was a *Local Hero* sort of place—which is why I keep returning.

The first tee is set just across the entrance road from the modest pro shop, and the opening eight holes run along an upper level of linksland that gives each one great character, whether as a result of the elevated tees or the angled approach shots, the sinister pot bunkers or the undulating greens.

The back nine begins on a lower level of ground that runs along the Dornoch Firth, and it provides golfers the chance to hit a mix of shots that test every aspect of their games: on the short par-three 10th and the longish par-four at 11, the wildly bunkered three-par at 13, and the meaty Foxy, No. 14, which Ross used as a model for holes he eventually built at Pinehurst and Seminole. A calm slowly rolls over me every time I play the track, as soothing and inebriating as a fine whisky on a cool day, and I long ago determined that if St. Andrews is the Home of Golf, then Dornoch is its Shangri-La.

Like Mac the oilman, I love it here, and I don't ever want to leave.

While I have teed it up at Dornoch on several occasions, I have yet to play Trump's course on the Aberdeenshire coast. But I have heard great things about it from golfing friends whose opinions I highly value. And not surprisingly, it is becoming a must-stop for anyone heading to that part of the world.

The Donald, whose mother, Mary MacLeod, grew up in Scotland and considered Gaelic her first language, opened his Trump International Golf Links in Aberdeen in the summer of 2012. Designed by Hawtree, a Scotsman whom the R&A

has commissioned to tweak several of its Open Championship venues, the course winds through giant sand dunes that offer stunning vistas of the North Sea. I am told that the fairways are wide and receptive, the revetted bunkers daunting yet fairly placed, and the greens set on natural ridges and tucked into tidy glens. With each hole having six sets of tees, it is guaranteed to be accessible to players of all abilities.

Not far from where Trump's mother spent her youth is a relative unknown layout called Askernish. And as I stood on a dune a hundred feet high overlooking the Atlantic Ocean on that track in the Outer Hebrides, I had to remind myself that I was actually on a golf course. Normally, that would not have been a difficult proposition given the setting, for the promontory on which I had just climbed features a coarsely mowed teeing area, and a somewhat shaggy fairway stretched below me to a far-off green. But this place felt different, even as I took a couple of practice swings and then smacked my drive into the cobalt blue sky.

That's largely because Askernish is as much archaeological dig as it is golf course. Originally built in 1891 by Old Tom Morris, the celebrated golf course architect from St. Andrews, it began to fall into disrepair after World War I. By the late 1930s, Askernish had disappeared, covered over by gnarly marram grass and buried by windblown sand. And while golf started being played again on the island of South Uist after World War II, it was on a crude, undistinguished layout constructed on a low-lying plain near the dunes where Old Tom had routed his original course. Morris's masterpiece had disappeared.

No drawings of Old Tom's layout were ever made, and no map of the holes he built at Askernish existed. But stories about the lost course abounded. Over the years they piqued the interest of local golfers as well as off-island aficionadas of the game, some of whom actually traveled the site. Among those making the trip was Scottish links consultant

Gordon Irvine; he became so enthralled with the proposition of restoring the Old Tom Morris track that in 2007 he and noted English golf course architect Martin Ebert took on the project. Working pro bono, they hiked endlessly through the dunes of Askernish, trying to reimagine and then re-create Old Tom's course. By August of the following summer, it opened for business.

Askernish had not only been unearthed, it had been brought back to life.

I remember thinking how thankful I was for that as I played Askernish a couple of times during a recent Scotland expedition, taking a short flight there from Inverness. Askernish has been described as the most natural golf course in the world, and it surely felt that way. The fairways, tees, and greens are casually maintained, to put it charitably. Cow pies and sheep droppings dot the grounds, which makes sense because this has long been common grazing property. There is no irrigation, and neither artificial fertilizers nor pesticides are used. Small daisies grow in such numbers on the fairway of the par-five 6th that it often looks as if it is covered with light snow, and one day I could not find the Pro V1 ball I hit for my drive even though I nailed it right down the middle. Two holes later, the ball from my tee shot rolled down one of the many rabbit holes on the property. At first, I was a bit miffed. But then I laughed, thinking the same thing probably happened to Old Tom, too.

It seemed at times that the only proper way to play Askernish was with hickory-shafted clubs and gutta-percha balls from Old Tom's era. But using the modern equipment did nothing to diminish the pleasure of this architectural treasure. It is a wild, rugged track to be sure, and probably best appreciated by those who fancy a good throwback and a place where the course is as historic as it is fun.

And there is plenty of history and fun to be had in Scotland's north and northeast.

6

PORTUGAL
Iberian Dream

THROUGH THE AGES, FOREIGNERS HAVE OVERRUN THE Iberian Peninsula, starting with the ancient Greeks and including in later years the Romans, Celts, and Moors. They were searching for economic gain (through trading) and political power (through the conquest of territory), and they often accomplished both of those goals. If only for a little while.

Centuries later, outsiders continue to pour into the land where modern-day Portugal is located. But the groups today are mostly coming to recreate, not ransack—and looking to repose in a place where the weather is generally warm and dry, the lifestyle laidback, the scenery in many cases spectacular, and the food and wine delightfully sublime.

Oh, and there also happens to be a lot of good golf.

Portugal is a sun-soaked land of only ten million people that is bordered by the Atlantic Ocean to the west and south and Spain to the north and east. I learned all I really needed to know about the nation the first night of my first visit there, when the fellow sitting next to me at a seaside bar on the country's Algarve Coast turned to me and said: "We are a very relaxed country. So it helps that you relax when you are here."

One week later, I understood just how right that fellow was, for Portugal is most definitely a place about kicking back.

I received my first lesson about the institutional imperative of that ethos almost as soon as I set foot in this land. Portugal was in the midst of a fiscal crisis so serious that a group of bankers and bureaucrats from the International Monetary Fund and European Union had come to see about renegotiating the country's massive debt. And the ruling government's response to that visit, which came just before Easter, was to give all federal workers an extra day off before the holiday weekend. So while the financiers tried to work out relief for a country that has long been living beyond its means, its citizens heeded the call of its leaders and deserted their jobs in droves.

I am sure that one of the reasons Portugal is that way is that there are so many places where people can go to take things down a notch. One option is lingering in a traditional coffee bar, or *pasteleria*, where the caffeine and camaraderie set a soothing social tone. Another is to venture to the beaches along the country's more than 1,100 miles of coastline. The vineyards of the Douro Valley are also a pretty good place to decompress, especially when glasses of wine made from grapes like Tinta Roriz and Touriga Franca are being poured. And so are the island getaways of the Azores and Madeira. Few places in this world are as good at washing away the worries of modern life than the port houses of Porto, the country's second largest city and the place after which this nation, which was founded in 1139, was named. Leisurely walks through the charming hillside barrios of Lisbon are quite good at bringing down the blood pressure, as are evenings in the fado bars of Portugal's capital, listening to mournful songs about the sea.

There is also the golf. The royal and ancient game is a fairly new addition to Portugal's vast menu of sporting activities. But in the years since British transplants like the three-time Open Champion and Ryder Cup stalwart Sir Henry Cotton introduced golf to that land in the 1950s, it has grown into an important diversion. Now there are more than eighty courses in the country, many of which are designed by architects like Robert Trent Jones Sr., Arnold Palmer, and Jack Nicklaus. They range in style and feel from rugged mountain layouts like Penha Longa to newer, scenic tracks near and along the cerulean Atlantic, such as Oceania Victoria and Oitavos Dunes. And developers continue to add to the country's golfing inventory, hiring other top architects, such as Tom Fazio and David McLay Kidd, to build new courses.

To be fair, golf is not the primary reason to make a trip to Portugal, for while this is a nation with golf, it is by no means a golfing nation. But the game certainly ranks among the most calming things to do in this land—followed, of course, by several hours spent on the beach or by the pool with a book and a beverage, and then a sumptuous seafood dinner.

Golf is concentrated about evenly in Portugal in two primary areas—the Algarve Coast that runs along the southernmost portion of the country and Lisbon, along the Atlantic to the north and east. The first courses to be laid out were mostly in the Algarve, a coastal region where people long made their living farming the land as well as the sea. Tourism is now the economic engine, and the area boasts a number of tight tracks that wind in and around red-roofed, white-walled houses and apartments, most of which are winter homes for northern Europeans (who treat this area the way Americans do Florida). One such track is San Lorenzo, which Joe Lee created in the late 1980s. The course runs through a section of the Ria Formosa Nature Reserve and along a tidal estuary that empties into the Atlantic. Its ample fairways are lined by stubby umbrella pines, and a round there not only features terrific ocean views but also the chance to hit a variety of shots from an array of angles. I was especially taken with the stretch of holes by said estuary, Nos. 5, 6, and 7. And I loved the vistas from the 12th tee of a sea-salt farm, with piles of that dietary staple being harvested the old-fashioned way, by shirtless men wielding wooden rakes in shallow rectangular pools.

The Royal Course at nearby Valle do Lobo is not nearly as roomy as San Lorenzo and more heavily lined with housing. But I find it as challenging and as fun, especially when we come upon the Atlantic on the 15th and 16th holes and get to watch and listen to the waves breaking against the rocky shore as we stand over our shots. Valle do Lobo was one of the first tracks built in the Algarve, which comes from the Arabic word meaning "the West" and harkens back to the time when the Moors ruled this part of Europe. The course has a bit of an older feel to it, which makes me think of Henry Cotton as I walk it and the trails he blazed in this area.

Oceanico Victoria is a completely different scene and represents another, very Americanized, version of golf that can be found in the Algarve. Located in the village of Villamoura and designed by Arnold Palmer, it is the site of the Portugal Masters, which Lee Westwood recently won. The course opened in 2004 and is flatter and brawnier than the others I played in the Algarve. And while it definitely has the ability to challenge the touring pro, it also gives the visiting golfer another way to enjoy the region—especially if he picks the right tees. I played from the Medal markers that measure about 6,600 yards on the par-72 track, and not only used every club in my bag but also relished the different shots I had to play, to say nothing of the sights of the olive grove off of the 4th green and the handful of horses I saw grazing on the grounds.

Outside Lisbon are the courses of the area known as the Estoril, just west of the nation's capital. One of the newest and best of that bunch is Oitavos Dunes in the seaside town of Cascais. Designed by Arthur Hills and opened in 2001, it is a links-style track overlooking the Atlantic to the south and the hilly forest of a national park to the north. The layout provides stunning views as well as an opportunity to play the game in its most traditional form—on the ground and in the wind. Purple and yellow wild flowers growing among the scrubby dunes enhance the visuals, as do the small coveys of perdiz, a sort of local partridge, scurrying across the fairways.

About an hour's drive from that layout is Penha Longa, a Robert Trent Jones design in the Sintra hills with 27 holes and a frequent host of the Portugal Open. A true parklands layout whose name translates into "Long Rock," it is set on a sumptuous estate on which Friar Vasco Martins built a monastery in the late 1300s and where members of the Portuguese royal family constructed opulent residences centuries later, as well as a palace. The course runs through shaded valleys and along rugged slopes dotted with groves of olive, eucalyptus, and cork trees. I have to hit many of my drives from elevated tees, and a number of my approaches to greens cut on the tops of small hills and are guarded quite capably by gaping bunkers. It is a tough routing, and also a scenic one. A seven-hundred-year-old aqueduct borders the 6th green, and the cupola of a fourteenth-century chapel is visible from the 18th tee. Between shots, I catch glimpses of the Atlantic Ocean, nearly ten miles away and pocked with white caps.

While a postround beverage on the terrace off the clubhouse at Penha Longa is always a good idea, I also find that a quick trip to the nearby town of Sintra is an even better thing to do when your golf is done. A town of just over thirty thousand people to the west of Lisbon, Sintra is full of lush parks, gaping gorges, and cobblestone streets. An eighth-century Moorish castle looms on a mountain ridge that is the highest point in Sintra, and visitors flock to the Pena Palace, which was built for the royal family in the 1840s from the ruins of an old monastery and features a drawbridge and ramparts as well as turrets and domes, and even a gargoyle above a Neo-Manueline arch. It is worth checking out those spots, and spending time in one of the town's coffee bars. Known as *pastelerias,* they serve strong Portuguese coffees called *bicas,* which are generally produced from Robusta beans harvested in Brazil, along with pieces of sweet, cinnamon-spiced cheesecakes called *queijada de Sintra,* or delectably crunchy custard tartlets known as a *pastel de nata.*

As good as the coffee is throughout the land, the food is even better. Outside Cascais, I discover the superb seafood joint Mar do Inferno. There, diners pick fresh fish from display cases and watch as waiters weigh their groupers and snappers and then take them into the kitchen to be cleaned and cooked. I ask for shrimp one evening and get a dozen, simply grilled with salt and lemon. I nod with approval when my waiter says, "No butter. It tastes better." Next, I order half a dozen langoustines, prepared exactly the same way, and I feel my eyes rolling in the back of my head as I wash them down with crisp white wine from the Alentejo.

I found the eatery O Jacinto in the Algarve village of Quarteira just as impressive, and the cooks there dish up the most savory seafood stews I have ever tasted, including one called *cataplana tamboril* that boasts monkfish, clams, and shrimp. Another must-visit is Sao Gabriel, which is located in Vale do Lobo and boasts one Michelin star. Sea scallops with braised pork belly were sublime as a starter, and a combination of lamb chops and leg of lamb with a bean cassoulet made the angels—to say nothing of my palate—sing. So did the tasty Esporao Reserva red wine from Alentejo in southwest Portugal I drank that night.

The Duarte Grill at the Dona Filipa Hotel in Vale do Lobo provided me with one of my most memorable meals in Portugal when I ordered an appetizer called *ameijoas a bulhao pato*, which are local clams cooked in their shells with white wine, garlic, and coriander, and followed that with grilled sole that was expertly filleted tableside. Years later I still dream about the scrambled eggs with crab and sea urchin that I ate in the hotel at Oitavos Dunes, and the melt-in-your-mouth smoked ham called *pata negra*, made from pigs that feast exclusively on wild acorns.

Another place where golfers should spend a couple of days is Lisbon, the Portuguese capital. And while there are no courses to be found in this bustling city of mostly white-walled buildings with reddish tile roofs and windows opening onto balconies ringed by cast-iron railings, there are plenty of good walks to take. None of which, by the way, can be spoiled by errant golf shots.

A couple of days in this metropolis of five hundred thousand people, which sprawls across seven hills and was more or less razed by an earthquake in 1755, also demonstrates that there are no shortages of things to do while, say, strolling down the wide, leafy Avenida Liberdade or hiking up the narrow, cobblestoned lanes of the Alfama *bairro*. Stop in a coffee bar to down a bracing *bica*, for example, and or take the time to savor a hoppy local beer called Super Bock in a sidewalk café as the men and women at adjoining tables converse in an array of languages. Spend a bit of time in some of Lisbon's city squares, where locals gossip as musicians play their guitars in the shade of tidy orange trees. Check out any number of the city's popular museums and galleries with works of art that tell the story of this scenic, seafaring city on the River Tagus that grew up around a trading post ancient Phoenicians are thought to have established around 1200 BC. Or soak up its sweeping views and the tempo of its different *bairros,* or neighborhoods.

The vistas from the aged ramparts of the Moorish citadel known as Sao Jorge Castelo in Alfama that loom over Lisbon are breathtaking, and it is worth taking the funicular up another of the city's formidable hills to tour the Bairro Alto, which fairly bustles with shoppers by day and clubbers at night. Another must is a trek to the Belem Tower just west of the city center; it is a fortified lighthouse dating back to the early 1500s, when Lisbon was Europe's hub of commerce and the one-time starting point for explorers setting out on journeys around the world. Belem also has the magnificent Jeronimos Monastery, which is one of the most noteworthy examples of the Manueline style of architecture so prominent in Lisbon. And do not forget the many fine eateries there as well, especially those specializing in the seafood brought in fresh each day from the nearby Atlantic.

They are terrific places to relax. As are the golf courses of this Iberian land.

7

PRESTWICK, TURNBERRY, AND MUIRFIELD

Open Gems

THERE IS SO MUCH GOOD GOLF IN THIS WORLD, AND players can find brilliantly designed courses on every continent, save Antarctica. But there is no place quite like Scotland. The game is thought to have been played there as long ago as the twelfth century, with sheepherders using crooks to bang stones into rabbit holes, stones dug from the sandy soil of the otherwise useless acreage linking productive farmland to the sea (hence the terms "links" and "linksland"). In addition, many of the greatest courses in the world are found in Scotland. As a result, it is regarded as golf's Holy Land, with thousands of players making pilgrimage there each year.

I have journeyed to Scotland on nearly two dozen occasions and believe it is the place where the royal and ancient game is enjoyed in its purest and most enjoyable form: On traditional courses with players carrying pencil bags holding only half-sets of irons and woods. At centuries' old clubs that possess more history than most museums. Across fairways where, since 1860, elite players have battled for the oldest and most coveted trophy in golf, the Claret Jug, which goes to the winner of the Open Championship. And in wood-paneled pubs afterward, where wee drams and frothy pints are shared postround.

There are several ways to organize proper golf trips to Scotland, and one of my favorites is to concentrate my play on places that have hosted the hallowed Open Championship. That's exactly what I did on my latest journey there, teeing it up on a trio of links layouts that have held multiple Opens and are among the finest and most historic golf courses in the world: Prestwick, Muirfield, and the Ailsa track at Turnberry. It was an enlightening tour that is in many ways the golfing equivalent of archaeologists trekking to ancient Greek or Roman ruins.

I began at Turnberry, a popular resort that real estate mogul and golf impresario Donald Trump purchased in the spring of 2014. Located in a town of that same name on Scotland's west coast in an area known as South Ayrshire, its Ailsa course has staged four Open Championships over the years. And while that track is hundreds of miles from the English town of Stratford-upon-Avon, I cannot help but think of it as Shakespearean for all the drama that has transpired in those tournaments. The first came in 1977, when Tom Watson edged Jack Nicklaus by a stroke in their famously fought "Duel in the Sun," winning with a birdie on the 18th hole. Nine years later, Greg Norman finally won his first major championship after multiple near misses, and in 1986, Turnberry was the site of Nick Price's one and only Open victory, by a mere stroke over Swede Jesper Parnevik. Then, there was the 2009 championship and one of the biggest heartbreaks in sports history, when Watson faltered on that same final hole after his seemingly perfect approach shot ran through the green and settled into very thick rough in back of the putting surface. Unable to get up and down, his bogey forced him into a four-hole playoff that was eventually won by Stewart Cink.

The Ailsa course, which was requisitioned by the military in both world wars and turned into an airfield, is also known for being as good a track as there is in Scotland. Hard on the water, with a rock outcropping known as Ailsa Craig rising like a massive dome from the firth eleven miles offshore, it is a marvelous melding of long and short holes with plenty of elevation changes, well-crafted bunkers, doglegs that bend both left and right, and persistent winds. Par is only seventy, and the course features but two par-fives, on Nos. 7 and 17. It is a tough track to be sure. But also fair and fun, and it compels players to be creative with their shots. Then there are the views, like those off the 9th and 10th holes, where a stately, white lighthouse built on the craggy coast looms by a thirteenth-century castle that is said to be the birthplace of the Scottish king Robert the Bruce.

Overlooking the course, on Bain's Hill, is the Turnberry hotel, an imposing structure that served as a military hospital during the world wars. It is an appealing place to stay so long as you don't mind big, and the views from the vast promontory on which it was built are stunning, especially as the summer sun sets on the waters of the firth below when dinner and after-dinner drinks are done.

Twenty miles by car to the north is the Prestwick Golf Club, with a classic links course that opened in 1851 as a 12-holer and an elegant stone clubhouse with a spacious sitting room that feels like an Edwardian library. Prestwick hosted the first British Open in 1860, when competitors played three loops in one day to complete what was then a 36-hole event. It has held a total of twenty-four Opens over the years, the last in 1925. The course is still used for major amateur events, but its strength these days is as a first-rate track for members and visitors. The 5th hole, dubbed Himalayas, is among the most famous par-threes in the game, and modern course architects have copied its blind tee shot over a mountainous dune to a green for decades. The par-four 17th, aptly named Alps for its towering dunes, requires a blind approach to a green guarded by a massive bunker called Sahara. That is as renowned a hazard as there is in the sport, and so is the Cardinal's Nob, a cross-bunker that bisects the fairway on No. 3 and is named in memory of a monk of the Crossraguel Abbey near Turnberry who once played a match to settle a deadly feud against a fellow golfer, the wager being the cardinal's "nob," or nose. The clubhouse provides a nice backdrop to the short par-four 18th, and I like how the green there, and the 1st tee, are just paces away from the main clubhouse entrance, a frequent feature of Scottish retreats that demonstrates the close connection between a club and its course, both visually and viscerally.

Prestwick is one of the most exclusive golf clubs in Scotland, but it happily welcomes visitors who possess valid handicaps. It is a treat and a true honor for traveling players to take advantage of that hospitality by teeing it up on such an esteemed track, and also by partaking of perhaps the most celebrated lunch in golf. Those are not modest repasts but rather extensive meals that begin quite delightfully with a Pimm's Cup or a Whisky Mac, which is a combination of whisky and Crabbie's Green Ginger Wine. This is followed by salad, meat, and vegetable courses as well as wines, cheeses, and desserts. Jackets and ties are required, lending a charming formality to the occasion, and seating is communal, which nurtures a pleasing sense of camaraderie among the dining golfers.

A little more than two hours' drive to the northeast of Prestwick is the region called East Lothian. While its farmland is among the country's most productive, the area is also rich in golf. And nowhere as much as in the small coastal village of Gullane. The Gullane Golf Club, founded in 1882, boasts three wonderful courses, simply named Nos. 1, 2, and 3. But the distinction of being the best course in town goes to Muirfield, home course of the Honourable Company of Edinburgh Golfers, which was founded in 1744. While the club itself is one of the oldest in the game, the actual layout on which its members play today only came to be in 1891. Initially designed by Old Tom Morris and revamped in 1923 by Harry Colt, it is sometimes described by locals, tongues firmly planted in cheek, as Gullane No. 4, for it is the newest of the four layouts in town. But no one ever mocks it for its superb routing and the way it exposes golfers to wind from every possible angle, with a front nine that runs in a clockwise direction and a back that goes counter. Alternate shot is the preferred mode of play, though fourballs are occasionally permitted. The club is not only among the oldest in Scotland—and the place where the first rules of the game were promulgated, but also arguably the most exclusive, with an air of power and panache not unlike that at Augusta National in the United States. While it is not easy for nonmembers to secure tee times at Muirfield, it certainly is possible do so on the two days a week that are open to visitors. And as is the case with Prestwick, the club is also happy to have guests stay for its lunches, which also are cheerful, somewhat boozy affairs, with diners clad in coat and tie. It is also worth finding the time to sip a wee dram in one of the public rooms in the clubhouse, all of which are adorned with vintage photographs, paintings, and golf memorabilia and feature picture windows that afford expansive panoramas of the golf course and Firth of Fore beyond.

Muirfield has hosted sixteen Open Championships, and the roster of victors from those competitions is an impressive one that lends even more prestige to the golf course. Jack Nicklaus won there, and so did Lee Trevino and Phil Mickelson. Nick Faldo was triumphant at Muirfield twice.

Next to the clubhouse at Muirfield rises one of the finest hotels in golf, Greywalls. Designed by the Edwardian architect Edward Lutyens in the early 1900s, it was built as a "dignified holiday home" and then converted into an inn with twenty-three sumptuous, en suite guest rooms. Oil paintings and prints depicting golfing scenes hang from the walls and porcelain pieces adorn shelves. Memorabilia is also on display from visits by past Open competitors, many of whom stayed there during the championships. Service is stylish, and the "snug bar" is a wonderful place to savor a postround whisky, as is the rather substantial walled garden.

Greywalls backs up to Muirfield, and as I stand on the hotel terrace that overlooks the golf course and the firth beyond, I think of the road signs I have seen at the outskirts of almost every village I have motored through on this trip. They read: "Haste ye back." Which is exactly what I intend to do.

8

LONDON

Across the Heathlands and along the Sea

IT USED TO BE THAT WHEN I CONSIDERED GOLF IN THE British Isles, I never thought of London. To be sure, the English capital has long been a favorite destination of mine, for its plays and parks and also the churches, galleries, and museums. When it came to teeing it up, however, I only saw London as a place to pass through on my way to golfing points farther north. Like Glasgow and Edinburgh. Or Shannon and Dublin.

But as I stood on the second floor veranda of the white-walled clubhouse at Royal Cinque Ports and gazed across the windswept links where Julius Caesar's Roman legions once marched, I realized I was now of a very different mind. I had just spent a week exploring the historic heathland courses just west and south of London. Then I played several rounds at this marvelous course on the English Channel, only ninety minutes by train from the city, and also at nearby Royal St.

George's. The tracks were excellent, the clubs as convivial as any I have ever known, and I could not help but ask myself: how did I miss this area for so long?

A day later my journey ended with a round on the Old Course at Sunningdale with John Baldwin, a part-time London resident and well-resumed golfer who has won the British, Irish, and Welsh Senior Ams. And I asked him the same question I had posed to myself the previous afternoon.

"Don't feel bad," he said. "London is a place that often is easily overlooked, and that's a shame, because it is one of the great golf regions in the world."

At the start of my trek, I would have found that last pronouncement difficult to credit, as the Brits might say. But hearing it at the conclusion, it made perfect sense. John was exactly right.

The track we had just played at Sunningdale, the rugged Old Course designed by Willie Park in 1901, is an architectural triumph routed through rolling hills and swathes of heather. I liked how the classic heathland track takes advantage of the well-contoured land and gives golfers a variety of angles on tee shots and approaches. And I appreciated the great variety in the length of the holes, with par-fours ranging from nearly 460 yards to just a tad over 260, and enjoyed the relaxing ethos of a place where many members play their rounds with their Labradors and spaniels in tow. Some dogs are tethered to their masters' pull carts, and the canine culture is so strong that the club leaves out dishes at water fountains, so both players and pups may quench their thirsts during rounds.

Though I did not get to play the second track at Sunningdale, dubbed the New and laid out nearly a century ago on similarly interesting terrain by Harry Colt (the first secretary in the association's history), club members told me it was just as good, if not better.

After our round, John and I ate dinner in a nearby eatery town at a pub called The Thatched Tavern; the four-hundred-year-old beam building reminded me of how charming and good an evening can be in Surrey. The savory lamb shanks fell off the bone, and the after-dinner plate of local cow, sheep, and goat cheeses worked brilliantly with the glass of vintage port (Dow 1963) that the owner so generously sent over. In fact, it was so tasty that we ordered another, and as I nursed that, I told John all about my golf the week before.

It had started with a game at nearby Swinley Forest, another Colt masterpiece where a few of the holes run along the ovals where Thoroughbreds are trained to run at Ascot, maybe the most celebrated racetrack in the world. Located just six miles from Windsor Castle, the massive, eleventh-century abode that serves as one of the residences of Britain's royal family, Ascot hosts twenty-six days of racing each season, including the week-long Royal Meeting in June, which is usually attended by Queen Elizabeth II and other members of her clan.

Founded in 1911, Swinley boasts only one par-five and a quintet of three-pars. It is also one of the most scenic layouts I have ever seen, with fairways lined by vast stretches of rhododendrons, their magenta blossoms making players feel as if they had walked into a Claude Monet painting. At first glance, the par-68 course looks like a cupcake, measuring a mere 6,019 yards from the tips. But Swinley is a tough layout, and you need to be a real shot maker to score there.

Next, I visited Worplesdon, which was routed in 1908 by J. F. Abercromby, with Willie Park Jr. handling the green designs and bunkering. The land here is replete with stretches of heather and copses of pines and broom, and I adored the way the back nine started, with a par-three, a pair of five-pars, and another par-three. A little less pleasurable, however, were the harrowing road crossings golfers must twice endure during a round there, and the near-death experiences that come from having to occasionally dodge cars and lorries that are speeding by.

Then there was the Old Course at Walton Heath, host of the 1981 Ryder Cup. Five-time Open Championship winner James Braid was the longtime golf professional at that club, Winston Churchill a member, and the Duke of Windsor served for a spell as captain. In describing that spot, the great British writer Bernard Darwin once wrote: "There is no more charming place on a fine sunshiny day, none where the air is fresher and more cheering, none where the sky seems bigger." He was also a big fan of the Old, and lauded it for the way it provided a feeling of playing a seaside links, with its frequent wind and firm fairways, even though it was an inland course.

My only regret during my time in that area was not finding the time to tee it up at Stoke Park, a club that features 27 holes designed by Harry Colt. His work there is highly acclaimed, but what really intrigued me was that the golf scene from *Goldfinger*, in which James Bond and Auric Goldfinger played a spirited match, was filmed there. Maybe next time.

One thing I did not miss was taking advantage of the off-course options that exist in an area so close to London. One evening, I hopped a commuter train to Waterloo Station in London. Half an hour later, I was in a cab, on my way to the Globe for a performance of *A Midsummer Night's Dream*. It was Shakespeare at his best, at a theater built near the site of the original Elizabethan playhouse that staged so many of the Bard's pieces in the early seventeenth century. Seeing one of his works there felt like the golf equivalent of teeing it up on the links of St. Andrews.

Once my time in the healthland was done, I headed east to the Kent coast, where Royal Cinque Ports and Royal St. George's are located. Deal, as the course at Royal Cinque Ports is known, is a classic out-and-back track frequently buffeted by stiff winds. Founded in 1892, it hosted Open Championships in 1909 as well as 1920, and was slated to have the tournament again in 1939 and 1949. But those last two opportunities were lost when the links was flooded by high tides. The course design alone makes Deal a must-play, and it was in superb shape when I visited, in large part because it was going to be the site of the British Amateur just three weeks later. And the club's history only enhances the experience. King Edward VII often played there in the early twentieth century and for two years served as club president. In later years, King George V and King Edward VIII were frequent guests. I also marveled at the sight of an old World War II machine gun turret on the course, which my playing partners called "the German clubhouse," as well as the road built by ancient Romans that runs through the property and is still in use. I also got a kick out of a pub called The Chequers located along that historic thoroughfare, just to the right of the 15th hole. The owners of the establishment hang a checkered flag outside to let people know when it is open. They see it as a service to club golfers who might be a tad thirsty, or inclined to leave the layout for the bar if they are having a particularly bad golf day.

Royal St. George's, aka Sandwich, is an equally impressive place, having been the site of fourteen Open Championships, thirteen British Ams, and a pair of Walker Cups. The course is open and treeless, with the holes running in all directions, meaning that players never have to grapple with the same wind for very long. Gnarly dunes give the land terrific character, and the pot bunkers quite ably protect par. Three thatched-roof starter huts by the first tee add a quaint flavor, and the spacious clubhouse feels like a golf museum, with its displays of trophies, framed scorecards, photographs, and other memorabilia that lay out the club's rich heritage.

It was a terrific place to tee it up, and one more reminder of how remiss I was not to play around London before.

I determined I would not make that mistake again.

9

WALES

A Kingdom's Hidden Gem

AS THE WELSH GOT READY TO HOST THEIR MAIDEN RYDER Cup in 2010, they liked to say it took eighty-seven years to bring that biennial competition to their golf-crazed country for the first time. But they might as well add that it has taken about that long for most of the sporting world to discover what a great destination that charming land of three million people is for those who fancy the royal and ancient game.

Prior to a late summer visit that year, I counted myself among the unaware, abashedly so. At that point in my golfing life, I had been to Scotland a dozen times over the years, and Ireland six. But I had never before visited Wales, which boasts 189 tracks, of which 22 are links.

Of course, it was the quality and variety of the golf there that surprised and enticed me most, layouts with lyrical names like Porthcawl and Pyle & Kenfig that are brilliantly designed and beautifully situated. They are parts of golf-centric clubs where the game is enjoyed in its most delightfully basic forms. Where the clubhouses are small and simple, the locker rooms charming if not a bit musty, and the members so hospitable they gladly share games and pints with perfect strangers (though no one stays a stranger for very long in Wales).

But there are many other allures for the golfer traveling to that country, which is roughly the size of Massachusetts. The scenery, which includes sweeping stretches of pale sand beaches, swathes of purple heather bending in the seemingly ever-present wind, and rugged hills that can be crowned with snow in winter, may be the first attraction. And while it can certainly rain and blow, the weather is so temperate in most places—and the drainage so good—that golfers can play year round.

Food is also a highlight in Wales, and I marveled at the flavor of its black beef and mountain lamb, the taste of the local butters and cheeses, and the salty freshness of its fish. The trips from farm and sea to table are very short, and I never stopped applauding the deft ways in which Welsh chefs served as middlemen in that process.

As for the people, they are as friendly as they are feisty, and fiercely proud of their country and heritage.

Friendliness seems a national trait. Fives times I went to tee it up by myself. And five times I ended up playing or finishing rounds with locals—and finishing pints in the clubhouse with them afterward. At Royal Porthcawl, I told the assistant pro I was going to nearby Pyle & Kenfig the next day. "I'm a member there," he said. "Would you mind if I joined you?"

The same thing happened at Saundersfoot, a town farther to the west. I was lounging around the lobby at the St. Brides Hotel, golf clubs and shoes lying nearby, when the hotel owner, Andrew Evans, stopped by to introduce himself and then asked where I was playing. "Tenby," I said, referring to the oldest club in Wales, founded in 1888 and set along the sea just a ten-minute drive away. "I'm a member there," he responded. "And I'd love to show you around."

As I played with Andrew that day, I asked why the Welsh are so welcoming. "Remember, we are Celtic, like the Irish," he opined. "Which means we are a warm people. A little shy and reserved at times, but very friendly and warm."

But I could see they are also a tough sort, something born from the ways they endured invasions and occupations centuries ago by the Romans, Normans, and Saxons. Equally as difficult was the longtime rule of the English, and the Welsh mettle was further strengthened by the hardscrabble living so many of them had to fashion in more modern times in dank coal mines and gritty steel mills. There was nothing easy or soft about any of that, but you never hear the Welsh complain. They simply keep battling.

"Our history has given us that fighting spirit, that sense of never backing down or giving up and that attitude that the little one will always give the big one a good scrap if he has to," Andrews said at Tenby. "Remember, we like rugby more than football, and certainly more than cricket. And we did hold off the Romans."

Suddenly, I thought of Ian Woosnam winning the 1991 Masters, vigorously pumping his fist when his final putt dropped. That image of the diminutive Welshman explained it all.

Fortunately, I found the golf courses I played in Wales just as rich in character as the people. Like Royal Porthcawl, which was founded a hundred years before Woosie's Augusta triumph and has been the site of six British Amateurs as well as the 1995 Walker Cup, in which the Great Britain and Ireland (GB&I) team whipped an American squad that included a young Tiger Woods.

Porthcawl takes golfers on an invigorating ride the first few holes along Rest Bay, where the steel-gray waters are covered with white caps, and then turns inland, with farmland full of cattle, sheep, and horses providing the new backdrop. The course is flattish, which means the sea comes into view on every hole, and not particularly long from the members' tees. But strategically placed pot bunkers keep players from going too low, as does the wind. It can blow here, and members like to tell about the time twenty years ago that a gale knocked over the ramshackle pro shop, scattering bits of the building in the parking lot. The clubhouse hardly looks more substantial, but it is a wonderfully unassuming spot that houses one of the best men's locker rooms in golf. The luscious wood paneling lends a soothing touch, while the photos of past captains going back more than a century evoke a sense of the club's rich history, as do the boards honoring tournament winners through the years. I parked myself in a leather chair there for a good thirty minutes during my visit, lager in hand, gawking at the sea through a picture window and at a handful of surfers trying to catch waves off a beach to the left.

Just a short drive away is Pyle & Kenfig, a course overlooking Royal Porthcawl and the Bristol Channel beyond, which should have two names because it has two very distinct nines. The front is what locals call a downland track, open and somewhat flat, firm and fast like a links, with pot bunkers swallowing up errant tee shots and guarding testy greens. But I entered a different world on the back, one of blind tee shots, calf-high rough, and towering dunes covered with ferns. It blew twenty knots, and I loved the challenges that side presented, especially when I hit a pretty good tee shot with my driver on the 201-yard par-three 12th and watched hopelessly as it was yanked by the wind into the gorse at least thirty yards to the right of the green. I never found it and lost three more balls before the afternoon was done. But I couldn't have cared less.

I relished the feeling of being lost among the hauntingly empty dunes and didn't even mind when a bit of rain started to fall as the wind picked up. That's because I had a warm and welcoming retreat waiting once the round was done—the Great House just ten minutes away in Bridgend. The small hotel is located in a stone building dating back to the fifteenth century and features a cozy bar with flagstone floors, oak beams, mullioned windows, and an inglenook fireplace. It also serves a superb Welsh whisky, called Penderyn, and I happily enjoyed a wee dram or two.

I felt just as exhilarated by my morning round the next day at Southerndown, a club that was started in 1905. I teed off in the rain by myself so early that the pro shop was still closed. So I had no scorecard or course map, and there were times I could barely see through the mist fifty yards in front of me. But I managed to see just enough to find fairways that undulated wildly and greens that were tucked in and around dunes. I thought I had never been as alone on a golf course as I walked the 4th fairway when I suddenly looked up to see a dozen sheep standing in front of me. I stopped, and as we regarded each other for a moment, I thought of a statistic I had heard the night before, about sheep outnumbering people in Wales three to one. I was definitely outnumbered here.

Tenby two days later was just as beguiling, and a whole lot drier, with tight fairways, gaping pot bunkers, and very short walks between greens and tees. The course runs along Tenby South Beach, so wind is often a factor here as well. But its proximity to Bristol Channel provides a constant array of water views, and I was particularly taken with the one of the monastery island Caldy from the 5th tee, its verdant hills and lush meadows looming just offshore. I also liked that several holes have shots so blind that preceding golfers have to ring bells after they hit to signal "All Clear" for those behind them.

While Tenby was the oldest course I played, the Ryder Cup track at Celtic Manor was by far the newest. Called the Twenty-Ten and laid out in the lush Usk Valley, it opened in 2007 and was built exclusively for the 2010 matches by billionaire telecommunications entrepreneur Sir Terence Matthews. Traditionalists will no doubt be disappointed that it is an American-style layout and not a links. But the Twenty-Ten was well conditioned, well designed, and certainly worth playing given its status as a Ryder Cup site.

A Ryder Cup, by the way, that had been a very long time coming.

10

SOUTHWEST IRELAND
On the Pilgrim Path

THERE ARE SEVERAL SOLID CIRCUITS AROUND THE WORLD for those who like to travel with their sticks, routes that lead golfers on tours of top-flight tracks located in specific areas and allow both on- and off-course adventures to unfold like well-structured novels. St. Andrews, Scotland, to be sure. Pinehurst, North Carolina, and the Sand Belt outside Melbourne, too.

Another noteworthy trek takes players on a stirring loop through southwest Ireland, with stops at some of the best links layouts in the world. Like the Old Courses at Lahinch and Ballybunion, and newer tracks at Waterville, Doonbeg, and Tralee. It's a well-worn pilgrim path trod by golfers who regard visits to one of the game's ancestral homes as religious experiences. For many of them, it is where they taste the historic links of the British Isles for the first time. Yet it is also a favorite destination for veteran voyagers, and a place they return to time and time again.

Southwest Ireland was the first part of the Emerald Isle I visited as a golfer, and I fell hard for the rugged links courses that wound through dunes and along estuaries and bays there, and the glorious sense of playing the game in its most traditional form. And I happily return to that region any chance I get.

I started my latest trip there with a day and night of rest at Dromoland Castle after my overnight flight from New York. Located on a 375-acre estate just eight miles from Shannon Airport, Dromoland once served as the royal seat of the O'Brien family, who were descendants of Brian Boru, the former High King of Ireland. Today, the sixteenth-century Gothic structure operates as a one-hundred-room hotel, and I lingered in my sumptuous suite for much of the morning and early afternoon before heading out to play the front nine of the parkland-style golf course that Irish golfing legend Joe Carr and American architect Ron Kirby laid out on the grounds. Later that evening I dined on luscious local lamb in the castle's elegant Earl of Thomond restaurant and afterward enjoyed an Armagnac in the Cocktail Bar, which feels like the Edwardian library it once was.

Not surprisingly, I felt quite refreshed when I rose the next morning and drove to nearby Lahinch, an austere, deftly routed seaside links that boasts a brilliant architectural pedigree, having been tweaked over the years by Old Tom Morris, Alister MacKenzie, and most recently, Martin Hawtree. It is as scenic as it is strategic, and the course also features two of my favorite golf holes. The first is the par-five 4th, dubbed Klondyke for the massive "Klondyke" dune that players must hit over with their second shots to a green that backs right up to a stone wall. Next is the fabled Dell hole, a short three-par to a green tucked behind a dune that obscures most of the putting surface. Those are tough plays, to be sure. But fun ones, too, especially when the wind is up. And they lead players to the best stretch of the track, to the Atlantic behind the 6th green, along those waters on the par-four 7th, and then back into the dunes for the par-three 8th, where the tee is set on bluffs overlooking the ocean.

The weather was sunny enough that Lahinch's famous goats were wandering the layout instead of hunkering down in hollows by the clubhouse, which is what they do when the rains roll in. But the steady wind kept things interesting by forcing me to make two- and three-club compensations on most shots and play the majority of my approaches on the ground. It is a true shot maker's track—which I love.

I headed to Doonbeg after that round, to play the course Greg Norman laid out more than a decade ago among coastal dunes that rise as high as one hundred feet. This four-hundred-acre retreat is located in a sleepy hamlet that has, in typically Irish proportion, one church and five pubs. It has become a must-stop for most golfing visitors, but some have even complained that Norman's design is impaired by environmental restrictions that limited where he could route his holes. The course also has something of an American feel to it, with fairway markers revealing distances to the middle of the greens, not to the fronts as is usually the case in the Old World, and measured in yards not meters. Visitors are also likely to see more golf carts here than at any other links in Eire.

That sense of a US presence is likely to grow now that Donald Trump owns Doonbeg. The New York real estate magnate bought it in the winter of 2014 and immediately engaged Hawtree to revamp the golf course. This is the same fellow who laid out Trump's celebrated track in Aberdeen, Scotland. Not surprisingly, the Donald also gave the retreat a new name: it is now the Trump International Golf Links

& Hotel Ireland. He assures one and all that when he and Hawtree are finished Doonbeg will have "one of the great golf courses in the world."

From there, I motored south to Ballybunion. Part of that journey entailed a soothing and timesaving ferry ride across the Shannon Estuary, and I thought of how the drives between courses here can be almost as enjoyable as the golf itself. Many of the passageways are narrow lanes bordered by mossy walls and hedges as high as minivans, and they take you by verdant fields full of cows and sheep and through tiny towns that look as if they have not changed for centuries. I savored the sights on either side of the road and didn't even allow myself to get upset when I got stuck behind sluggish forty-year-old tractors and horse-drawn carriages, or had to stop so farmers could move herds of livestock across the road from one pasture to another.

Remarkably, after several trips to southwest Ireland, this was going to be my first round at Ballybunion. And I thought of how Tom Watson once told me that it took him a long time to really like links golf. In fact, it wasn't until after he won his third Open Championship, in 1980, that he began to feel comfortable on those often quirky tracks. He allowed that the transformation came when he played the Old Course at Ballybunion for the first time. That certainly spoke to the quality of that links, and it made me pine for many years to play there.

I was not disappointed, especially when I got to the par-four 7th, which runs along the Atlantic, and had to hit my drive from a dune set high above a beach that is as wide as a polo field is long. Even better was No. 11, another four-par with a towering beachside tee and a panorama that caused my pulse to quicken and my eyes to widen. As I prepared to drive, I aimed for a landing area that was backed by tall, grassy dunes, and when my golf ball settled in the middle of the fairway some 230 yards away, my caddie told me that the hole was named "Watson." For Tom, of course.

But the best part of the day came when I managed to ace the par-three 8th, with an eight iron from 140 yards. After the round, I bought drinks for the other members of my foursome in the clubhouse bar. And I could not help but think of the man who inspired me to come to Ballybunion. The next time I see Tom Watson, I promised myself, I have to tell him all about my hole in one here.

My following stop was Waterville, and as I drove along the coast I gawked at the hills that loomed to the east, either brilliant green with stretches of gorse and its flecks of yellow flowers, or tawny colored from swathes of heather not yet in bloom. I also checked out the seas, bays, and inlets and savored the smell of salt water that wafted through my open car window and that of peat logs burning in the fireplaces of nearby homes. I had to stop on a couple of occasions, for herds of cattle and sheep that were ambling down the pavement in no apparent rush. But that didn't bother me, for I was not in any hurry either.

While Ballybunion was a first-time experience for me, Waterville was like going home, for I know the place well, thanks to my friend Jay Connolly. An American investment banker who bought the golf course in the late 1980s with several colleagues from the financial services industry, he has helped to transform it into one of the finest tracks in all of Ireland.

Waterville had opened as a 9-hole course in 1889, and operated mostly for workers who had come to the town to construct and then maintain one of the first trans-Atlantic cable stations. The links was well used for several decades but then shut down in the late 1950s as the need for cable communications ebbed. An Irish American named John Mulcahy bought the property in the 1960s and induced the late architect Eddie Hackett as well as the then Winged Foot golf professional—and former Masters champion—Claude Harmon to build an 18-hole track on that same site. The new layout opened in 1973, and after Connolly and his gang became owners, they brought in Tom Fazio to revamp the layout yet again.

This resulted in a superlative course with a compelling mix of holes and shots as well as some remarkable vistas of the Atlantic and the surrounding mountains. Gary Player has described the 11th there as "the most satisfying par-five of them all," and Raymond Floyd once selected Waterville as one of his five favorite courses on earth. I could not agree more with both declarations and would only add that there is nothing quite as unique and good in golf as the Mass Hole, which is No. 12. A tidy par-three, it plays into dunes where local Catholics once risked their lives by holding secret services.

Another of the pleasures of that spot is Waterville House, a charming eighteenth-century manor that was once Mulcahy's home and is now owned by the same fellows who hold the golf course. It features ten guest rooms as well as a common room that is as comfortable a place to enjoy a postround beverage as can be found in golf. The house overlooks the Atlantic and abuts the famed Butler's Pool, one of the best salmon fisheries in Ireland. Longtime Waterville resident Charlie Chaplin fished there frequently, and so have Tiger Woods, Mark O'Meara, and Payne Stewart, as they often stayed at Waterville House—and played the nearby golf links—during pre–British Open golf trips.

After a couple of days in Waterville, I traveled to another course I had never played before, the Old Head Golf Links in County Cork. To be fair, I had heard mixed reports on this course, which was designed in part by Hackett, Kirby, and Carr on a windswept promontory that juts some two miles from the mainland into the Atlantic Ocean. The reports more or less sounded the same. Spectacular locale; ho-hum design. So I expected to be underwhelmed, but what I received instead was a wonderful surprise.

After a few holes, I felt as if I was playing on top of the world, and the presence of a Turnberry-esque lighthouse at the southernmost tip of the property only enhanced the sense of being somewhere special. So did the stretches of water that are almost always in view and the sight of seabirds soaring *below* me as I hit drives from the edges of cliffs. Many of the par-fours felt like the 8th at Pebble Beach, with their rocky crags, roiling seas, and heaving fairways, while most of the par-threes reminded me of the fabulous 12th on the Straits Course at Whistling Straits in Wisconsin, the greens fairly hanging on precipices. To be fair, not every hole knocked me out. But the vast majority elicited oohs and aahs from the members of my foursome, and as we sipped stouts in the clubhouse afterward I could not help but think that it isn't any wonder golfers keep coming back.

11

SWITZERLAND AND ITALY

Continental Delights

WHILE I AM A NEW ENGLANDER BY BIRTH, I AM IN MANY
ways a European in spirit. I have lived, worked, and studied
on the Continent for years and wandered around many of
its countries, endlessly enamored of the varied people and
cultures I encountered along the way and the mélange of
languages I heard, some of which I learned to speak. I also
adored the interesting places I was able to see, from modern
museums to ancient ruins, alpine meadows to Mediterranean
beaches, and everything in between. It was the diversity of
those lands that I relished as well as the timeless sense of history and the feeling of trekking such well-worn and worthwhile paths. I cherished the discoveries I made. Whether it
was a local seafood dish or a native artisan or a glass of wine
at dusk that tasted of the very herbs and flowers and soil I had
been smelling in the air the entire day.

Switzerland and Italy are my favorite countries on the Continent, and that no doubt stems from my having lived on several occasions in Ticino, the Italian-speaking canton of Switzerland. It was there that I developed an affection for the many similarities of those nations as well as their numerous differences—and the ways that their characters meld so well, the charming efficiency of the button-downed Swiss complementing the *gusto* of the devil-may-care Italians.

As a result, Italy and Switzerland are terrific places to tour and explore, as a visitor and a resident. And I was pleased to figure out that they also have some very good things to offer the traveling golfer.

To me, Switzerland has long been a place about secrets. Its banking laws for many years served as a sort of international symbol of financial furtiveness. Not to mention the stories of its military "reduit" I heard when I lived in that alpine land, the ones describing how the Swiss hid massive airfields in mountains and concealed powerful artillery cannons throughout the countryside as part of a grand civil defense strategy should the country ever be invaded.

After residing again in that European nation of nearly eight million people, I learned another little secret about Switzerland. It also happens to be a pretty good golf destination. Not on par with Scotland or Ireland, mind you, or Pinehurst or Pebble Beach. But it certainly merits a visit if you like playing scenic, well-conditioned courses routed high in the hoary crags of the Alps or along deepwater lakes lined with palm trees—and savoring a very Continental lifestyle along the way.

Consider the semiprivate Golf Club Crans-sur-Sierre. Located on a high plateau in the wine-producing canton of Valais in the western part of the country, with slate-gray, shark-tooth-shaped mountains rising all around, it boasts the best of the country's roughly sixty layouts. The par-72 track was built in 1924 on land where local farmers had long grazed their herds of cattle and was revamped a decade ago by Seve Ballesteros, its narrow fairways cutting through fir forests and across rolling plains to small, mostly crowned greens. And it fairly bustles throughout the golf season, like an alpine St. Andrews, with players toting their bags through town to and from the course.

Standing at the first tee at Crans-sur-Sierre, I ask my partner about my line. "Aim it at Mont Blanc," he suggests, and I chuckle at the instructions to use the highest of the Alps, its jagged dome covered with snow and ice even in the middle of summer, as my landmark. "I feel like I am hitting into *Heidi*," I say, admiring not only that imposing peak but also the neat terraces of Chasselas and Gamay grapes that ripen on the hills and the clusters of chalets that look almost like gingerbread houses spilling into the Rhone Valley below. Then I hear the sound of cows grazing in mountain meadows, the bells they wear from their necks clanging in the crisp afternoon air.

I learn during my round that the cattle of Crans-sur-Sierre are prized for the superb raclette cheese produced from their milk as well as for a delectable dried meat called "*vivende sechee*," both of which go very well with the excellent white and red wines made in that region. The town is also known as one of Europe's best ski resorts, a stylish retreat with streets full of Ferraris and Bentleys and stores selling Gucci and Hermes. Not surprisingly, it is a place where none other than Roger Moore, James Bond himself, calls home.

Crans-sur-Sierre is also a spot very much about golf. It hosted its first Swiss Open in 1939, and by the early 1980s that event had evolved into the European Masters, which takes place there each fall. Touring pros love the picturesque layout, and I can well understand why Greg Norman once described it as "the most spectacular tournament site in the world." I can also see why Adam Scott and Sergio Garcia bought homes there, just short walks from the first tee.

Crans-sur-Sierre also has one of the best *après-golf* scenes I have ever seen, and I take my lunch on the terrace outside the clubhouse whenever I am there, sipping a crisp Fendant from a nearby winemaker and nibbling on local cheeses and dried meats as I gaze at majestic Mont Blanc and listen to golfers at nearby tables chatter about their rounds in three or four languages. Once I am done with my meal, I usually exchange my FootJoys for a pair of hiking boots and trek partway up the mountain that serves as a ski area in the winter. Switzerland is a nation of walkers, and I generally pass several men and women on the trails that wind through the hills. I also see herds of cattle, and that reminds me of how farmers have grazed their cows on these slopes for centuries, moving them up and down as the snow lines rose and fell. Finishing up at sunset, the ice and snow on the Weisshorn in one direction and Mont Blanc in another turning a pinkish white, I am known to stop by a small restaurant across the street from the first tee. It has a Spanish theme and is only a few minutes' walk from Sergio Garcia's place. Invariably, I hear laughter inside and see there are a couple of golf bags leaning against the wall right outside the door. So I lay mine up against the wall as well and head inside for another Fendant.

Not surprisingly, the site of the European Masters gets most of the golfing attention in town. But I am just as taken with a charming 9-hole track just across the street that Jack Nicklaus redesigned in the late 1980s. The first tee is set behind a row of chalet-style apartments, and I feel as if I have stepped around a movie façade of a prototypical Swiss town. The course winds through a hilly section of woodland that gives players a chance to test their precision as golfers, for the 3,000-yard layout is all about accuracy and putting drives and approach shots in just the right places.

Golfers will also find a very enjoyable pair of courses to play in the Ticino, which is the southern-most region of Switzerland. Neither course has the dramatic vistas of Crans-sur-Sierre, nor the overall deftness of a design that is good enough to attract a European PGA Tour event. But they provide panoramas that are easy on the eyes as well as a number of well-crafted holes.

The finest of those layouts is found at Golf Club Lugano. A semiprivate retreat built on eighty acres just outside that Swiss city of forty thousand in the heart of the country's temperate lake region, it feels as much like an arboretum as a golf retreat, with its stands of palms and birches, ginkgoes and cedars. Rows of luscious merlot grapes running up and down fields that border the layout remind golfers that the Swiss make some tasty wine here as well, and the sound of the Magliasina River snaking through the middle of the course, which was built in 1923 and remodeled a decade ago by former Robert Trent Jones associate Cabell Robinson, provides a soothing sense to a round. So do the vistas of the gentle alpine foothills, all of which are dotted with villages that consist mostly of stone buildings with red-tile roofs. One day on the course, I discovered a stone shrine the size and shape of a house window. Called a "capella" and located just off the club grounds, it stood about six feet high and had a weathered fresco of the Madonna painted on the front. And the first time I walked up the 12th hole on the par-71, 6,200-yard layout, I came across an ancient Roman wall bisecting the hole. The club pro said forces occupying the area more than two thousand years ago had built it.

An equally enchanting option about an hour's drive away is Golf Club Patriziale in Ascona, a small town of five thousand residents famed for its annual music festival and set on Lake Maggiore near the Italian border. Palm trees flourish along its quiet streets, and outdoor cafés fairly bustle with locals drinking coffee laced with grappa, also known as *café corret-tos*. Originally a 9-hole track, Golf Club Patriziale opened just after Lugano, in 1928. The great British architects Colt and Alison redid the layout in 1932, and nine more holes were added in 1957. The result is a testy course that lies hard on the lake and evokes that wonderful sense of playing in a park.

Like Crans-sur-Sierre and Lugano, Ascona is as much about the setting as it is the score on the card. They combine with a number of other first-rate layouts to make golf another of Switzerland's secrets—and one the country is only too happy to share.

Knowing I have visited Italy a few dozen times over the years, a friend recently asked what I liked most about that European land.

"The food and wine," I blurted, even though that seemed such a pedestrian way to describe the pleasures of, say, a luscious Brunello and a plate of *cavatelli al pesto* so fragrant the aromas ignite the salivary glands the way a blasting cap sets off explosives. I also mentioned museums and ruins, of course, like the Uffizi in Florence and the Forum in Rome; the Alps and the lakes, too, especially around Como and Garda, when palm trees rise in the shadows of snowy peaks. Then, there are the people. *Dio mio, il populi*. As friendly and loving of life as any on this planet. And their language is so delightfully lyrical and spoken as much with the hands and eyes as the mouth.

"Did I mention the food and wine?" I asked only slightly tongue in cheek, and my friend laughed. Then he followed up with another question, an obvious one for anyone who knows me.

"What about the golf?"

Not too long ago, I could not have answered that question accurately because I had never teed it up in Italy. But I recently visited a couple of golf resorts there—Verdura in

Sicily and Palazzo Arzaga near Garda in the north—and that allowed me to provide a somewhat informed response.

The golf is good, I said. *Molto buono.* Not as extraordinary or wide-ranging as the food and wine, or as impressive and deep as the antiquities, but fun and enjoyable just the same, and one more way to absorb the pleasure and sense of being in Italy.

Admittedly, Italy is not a leading golf destination, and never will be. But I wasn't looking for another Scotland. Rather, I simply wanted to play some good courses, and to do so in a land full of character and fun.

I also wanted to check out a place whose countrymen were suddenly making noise in the professional golf world, and who were generating a lot of excitement in a nation where only one in seven hundred people tee it up (as compared to one in fifteen in Scotland)—and where soccer is still very much king. Two of those golfers were the *fratelli Molinari*—Edoardo and Francesco—Ryder Cup players who are now ranked among the top twenty in the world. Another was young Matteo Manassero, who had won the 2009 British Amateur and then a couple of European PGA Tour events after he had turned pro.

I started my tour in Sicily. Raw, rugged Sicily, the largest island in the Mediterranean with its endless orange and olive groves, its sunbaked villages, and its history of being overrun by invaders of every ilk, be they Greeks or Romans, Vandals or Goths, Arabs or Normans, French or Spaniards. Sicily appears to be something of a hard place as a result, and with very hardy people. But these are a people who have never lost their hospitality. No matter how many visitors may have conquered Sicily, Sicilians welcome visitors with open arms.

They certainly made me welcome at Verdura, the newly opened golf resort developed by luxury hotelier Sir Rocco Forte. Set on 570 acres just outside the historic fishing village of Sciacca and hard on the Mediterranean, it boasts a pair of superb 18-hole courses designed by Kyle Phillips, who built fabulous Kingsbarns outside St. Andrews. Phillips has created a similarly linksy layout here that features plenty of pot bunkers and favors those who can play the ground game. I liked the different angles the two Verdura courses compelled me to play and fancied the vast size of the greens, the ample width of the fairways, the varied lengths of the holes themselves, and the fact that I used every club in my bag. Water came into view throughout the rounds, providing enticing backdrops to several approach shots. Coupled with the seemingly ever-present wind, it also evoked a real sense of the British Isles. Until, that is, I realized the water up north doesn't turn so many different shades of blue and green. But this was the Mediterranean, not the Firth of Forth. And I appreciated even more deeply that I was in Sicily when I gazed up at the rocky hills towering over Verdura and the terraced vineyards rising like earthen stairs. It was hard not to think *Godfather II* when I did that. The opening funeral procession. Michael walking through the fields with his bodyguards. That association got even stronger when I considered that the village of Corleone was about an hour's drive away. I sometimes felt I could almost hear the music from that movie.

My days at Verdura quickly took on a pleasing rhythm during my stay there. Most mornings began with breakfast at the poolside restaurant, with a stout double espresso, sweet juice from oranges harvested from nearby groves, and a traditional Sicilian breakfast dish called Salsiccia, which consists of a char-grilled fennel sausage and a piece of toasted Italian bread drizzled with local olive oil and fresh oregano. Then, I headed to one of the golf courses for a round, followed by an afternoon lolling on the beach. I read on a lounge chair set under a thatched umbrella, and then waded into the salty sea for dips before heading to the beachside eatery called

Amare for lunch, where I dined on small, savory shrimp from Sciacca and an *insalata caprese* made of sinfully creamy Buffalo milk mozzarella; warm, ripe tomatoes picked that morning in Corleone; and extra virgin olive oil that is silky smooth and the color of gold. The food, and a perfectly chilled bottle of Planeta rose produced from grapes grown just down the road, made an afternoon nap an imperative. And then it was time for a bit of touring.

One day I drove to Agrigento, half an hour away. The coastal city is home to the Valle dei Templi, a collection of temples built in the Doric style during the fifth and sixth centuries BC in honor of the Greek gods. The ruins are so highly valued that UNESCO has named them a World Heritage Site—and are regarded as some of the largest and best-preserved ancient Greek buildings outside of Greece. I wandered around for a spell, gawking at the towering columns and lingering outside structures dedicated to Zeus, Juno, and Hercules, all facing east so they were illuminated at sunrise.

It was time for supper by the time I returned to Verdura. Though my cultural appetite was sated, I was nonetheless ready for a bit of dinner at another of the resort's restaurants, Liola. Set on top of a cliff overlooking the sea, it is named after the main character in a play written by dramatist Luigi Pirandello, who won the 1934 Nobel Prize for Literature and lived for years in a village outside Agrigento. Locally caught swordfish topped with more Corleone tomatoes as well as olives and capers was the special, and I dove right in, with waves breaking gently against the rocks below.

I could have stayed at Verdura for weeks. But I was also glad to move on to Palazzo Arzaga, which was just as appealing even if it could not have been more different. Located in the lush, rolling hills west of Lake Garda in Northern Italy, the pair of golf courses there wind through oak woodlands and around a restored fifteenth-century mansion and its private chapel, which is decorated with five-hundred-year-old frescoes. Leafy plane trees with their dappled bark line cobblestoned drives. Goats and cows graze in nearby fields. The Dolomites rise to the east, snow covering their highest peaks even in the middle of summer. And to the north is a quarry from which white Botticino marble is still cut.

There are 27 holes at Palazzo Arzaga. Jack Nicklaus II designed the first 18 very much in the parklands style, with wide, mostly tree-lined fairways and deep, grass-faced bunkers. Aged church towers dot the landscape around the course, their bells ringing hourly. When I started my round one Saturday morning, I noticed mine was the first tee time of the day. At 9 a.m.! And no one else was on the course—including members of the green staff, who didn't start showing up until 10.

Now, that's what I call casual golf!

The Nicklaus course opened in 1998, and a year later the resort brought a new 9-hole layout on line. Gary Player served as architect for that track, and his goal was to create a sort of inland links with riveted bunkers to complement Jackie's work—and to give the golf some variety. I found Player's to be a charming and equally pleasurable course that demanded a wide repertoire of shots if you had any hopes of scoring well. I had to hit fades and draws, lob wedges and bump-and-runs, and its quiet isolation gave me the sense of playing my own private course, or at the very least the course of a golf-obsessed Italian count.

As I hit the Player course one last time, I could not help but think of my friend who had asked me earlier this year about golf, Italian style. And I was happy to stick with my original answer.

Molto buono, indeed.

THE NEW WORLD

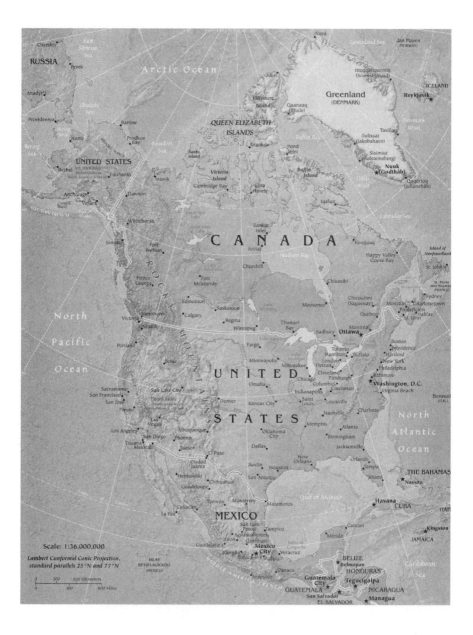

12

PEBBLE BEACH
California Dreaming

I'VE ALWAYS THOUGHT OF CALIFORNIA AS A PLACE THAT has it all. Part of that stems from my being a child of the 1960s and growing up when it was famously regarded as the Golden State, with sun-soaked beaches and endless summers of surf. And, of course, there was the artistic precociousness that makes California seem a cultural step ahead of the rest of the country. That was especially true with the music that flowed from there in my youth, as bands like the Beach Boys, the Grateful Dead, Jefferson Airplane, and the Doors produced songs that evoked all that seemed good and cool in the world.

My sentiments of California exceptionalism only grew as I came to better know that land in later years. I was particularly taken by the state's natural splendor as I toured its sumptuous vineyards and trekked among its redwood groves. I became smitten by stylish cities like San Francisco and besotted with eateries like Chez Panisse that set new trends in freshness,

technique, and taste. And I came to believe even more deeply
that in all those ways, California was extraordinarily beautiful and bountiful—and also a little better, a little richer, a bit
more special than anyplace else.

I was recently reminded of those feelings as I ate lunch
on the porch of the Stillwater Bar and Grill at the Lodge at
Pebble Beach. The cloudless sky was a mesmerizing blue, and
the 65-degree ocean air soothed my skin as seals and sea otters
swam across the cerulean cove before me. I nursed a glass of
Shafer Merlot (from California's wine country, of course) and
relished a salade Niçoise (with locally caught tuna) as I also
admired the verdant fairways of the Golf Links and the Santa
Lucia Mountains, their tops covered by wispy clouds.

Once again, I was in the California of my dreams. And
what made this particular dream better than most was that
I was about to play Pebble Beach, home to the old Crosby
Clambake and the current AT&T National Pro-Am. It's also
been host to numerous US Opens and Amateurs, and is inar-
guably one of the finest layouts in the land.

The town of Pebble Beach is one of the most beguiling
spots on earth, a scenic supermodel at which no sane soul can
stop gawking. The resort that was founded there in the early
twentieth century, with its swank hotels, state-of-the-art spa,
superb restaurants, and otherworldly golf, is just as fetching.

The main attraction for most is the Pebble Beach Golf
Links, and it was the creation of Samuel Morse, a cousin
of the man who invented the telegraph. A sportsman who
adored the spectacular beauty of the Monterey Peninsula,
he purchased seven thousand acres of land there in 1915,
including seven miles of oceanfront property. Morse set aside
the best parcels of that for a golf course, and then hired two
of California's top amateur players, Jack Neville and Douglas
Grant, to lay it out. The track opened for play in 1918, and it

initially played so tough that Morse closed it down for a spell so that the two designers could soften it up a bit.

Though the Pebble Beach Golf Links has undergone numerous nips, tucks, and tweaks since then, it has never lost its dynamic feel. The layout gently eases players into their rounds with a trio of modest holes. Then, it takes golfers on one of the most compelling stretches in golf, and provides some of the most exciting shots in the game. Like the second on the par-five 5th, up the massive hill with cliffs falling into Stillwater Cove to the right. Or the downhill tee shot at the par-three 7th, waves crashing against the jagged rocks behind the well-bunkered green. And the anxiety-inducing approach from the bluff on No. 8 that must clear a gaping chasm. Then, there is the mid-iron most players must hit into No. 9, and the Zen-like focus they need to stay down on their balls and not look up too fast to see it rise into—and then tumble from—the brilliant sky, with the spacious Carmel Beach laid out beyond.

Things drop down just a notch as golfers head inland on the 11th and begin working their way along a verdant ridge back home. But they rise back up when players get to the par-three 17th and start thinking of incredible shots hit there, Jack's one iron and Watson's wedge to be specific, as they also wonder how they are going to hold a ball on that testy, seaside green. Of course, the sweeping par-five that is No. 18 comes next, all dogleg and danger down the left side, putting the perfect bow on a damn near perfect course.

I would happily play Pebble Beach every day I am in town. But I'd also like to tee it up at the resort's other layouts. The Robert Trent Jones Sr.–designed Spyglass Hill is a wonderful layout that takes golfers on a marvelous ride from the Del Monte Forest to holes constructed among the sand dunes and then leads them back into the trees. It is laid out on land

Robert Louis Stevenson was said to have wandered as he wrote *Treasure Island.*

Not far from there is the Links at Spanish Bay. Created by Tom Watson, Sandy Tatum, and Robert Trent Jones Jr. in 1987, it never gets the acclaim of the other two. But it is a charming challenge overlooking the Pacific Ocean and 17-Mile Drive. And though I am not much of a range rat, I do enjoy heading to the short game area built among the dunes at cocktail hour, with my 60-degree wedge in one hand and an adult beverage in the other, as a bagpiper begins playing a mournful dirge that I can just hear above the roar of the waves a few hundred yards away.

If there is time, I also recommend a loop around the Del Monte Golf Course. Opened in 1897 and measuring only 6,365 yards from the tips, the par-72 layout with the small greens and wide, tree-lined fairways is the oldest continuously operating course west of the Mississippi River. It is also a favorite among locals, among them my caddie at Pebble Beach, who invited me to join him for a game at Del Monte during my latest journey there after we had finished on the big course.

While golf is the main attraction at Pebble Beach, it is by no means the only thing to do. The golfer's massages I often take at the resort's 22,000-square-foot spa, which features twenty-one treatment rooms, make me feel significantly younger than I actually am. Especially in the midst of a golf binge. And they do wonders for my swing by loosening up all the essential muscles. I also like visiting the Pebble Beach horse stables for trail rides through the section of the Del Monte Forest that runs between Spyglass Hill and Cypress Point and down to the Pacific Ocean, which gives me another perspective of that place.

On occasion, I also play at the Pasatiempo Golf Club, just forty-five minutes away. Marion Hollins, the former US

Women's Amateur champ who helped Alister MacKenzie design the fabled and ultraprivate Cypress Point Club course, founded Pasatiempo in 1929. She and MacKenzie had homes on the property, which is located in the college town of Santa Cruz, and they frequently played the rugged track, whose undulating fairways were designed to resemble those of the Old Course in St. Andrews and whose greenside bunkering is so evocative of MacKenzie's work at Cypress, Augusta National, and Royal Melbourne's West Course. The overall routing is strong, and so are the many views of Monterey Bay that come into play during a round, beginning with the elevated tee on No. 1. MacKenzie once declared the 16th at Pasatiempo to be "the best two-shot hole I know," and critics understandably rank the layout among the finest classic courses in the country. So does LPGA legend Juli Inkster, who grew up playing there.

Another worthy option even closer to the resort is the Pacific Grove Golf Links, a charmingly funky public course in a charmingly funky town of the same name. The scenic front nine begins with a pair of par-threes and winds through groves of cypress trees, playing firm and fast like a Scottish track. Then, the back nine heads to the sea, where the views of crashing waves and jagged rock outcroppings and fishing boats cutting through roiling water are as stunning as the breezes are strong. This part of the course is often dubbed the "poor man's Pebble Beach," and it is a good analogy. Pacific Grove is certainly not as well designed or as well maintained as the five-time US Open site. But it is still a wonderful place to play, and at less than $50 for a round, the price is right.

It is also yet one more reason to dream about golf in California.

13

KOHLER
The World of
Golf in One Place

IT'S DAY THREE OF MY LATEST TREK TO KOHLER, AND I think I've finally figured it out. Not my golf swing, mind you, which is as indecipherable as a teenager, and as helpless as one without an iPhone. Rather, I have come to understand why I like playing golf at this retreat so much.

I am walking onto the elevated tee on the 12th hole of the Irish Course when the revelation comes. It appears after I gaze down the right side of the par-four dubbed Highland Trek and see stretches of rugged dunes covered with brown-yellow grasses shimmering in the wind. Beyond is Lake Michigan, its waters so vast they feel as big as the North Sea. There is also a cluster of gnarly bunkers by the fairway and a small flock of black-faced sheep grazing nearby. When I turn to my left, however, I get a completely different visual, with brawny barns and glinting silos rising above fertile fields of corn and alfalfa.

Such dramatic contrast and such outrageous melding of new and old golfing worlds might put some players off. But I realize a definite delight in having both types of settings in one place. American farmland and Irish linksland. The modest Midwest and the Emerald Isle. Two of my favorite places in the world, and two of my favorite types of terrain. Here in Kohler, you get them both. On one golf course, as is the case with the Irish. And at one resort, with the links-style Straits track that sits hard on Lake Michigan. As well there are River and Meadow Valleys, courses at Blackwolf Run that wind through woods and across meadows, by farms, and along the Sheboygan River.

The scion of a privately held company founded in 1873 a century ago and best known for its plumbing products, Herb Kohler did not intend to create such disparities when he began constructing courses here in the late 1980s. His first two tracks, at Blackwolf Run, had very similar feels. But when he built the Straits, he decided to present his golfers with a very different option, a links-like track that evoked the great seaside courses of Ireland. Suddenly, players who came to Kohler had a distinct choice of golfing styles—and the opportunity to experience both in one day. With the opening of the Irish Course, not on Lake Michigan but within view of it, Kohler provided those possibilities on the same 18-hole track.

I like having these options, I say to myself as I contemplate my tee shot on the 12th. I like the range of auras, the different settings and senses. And I understand for the first time how those provide an enticing variety and completeness to the golf experience here that sets it above most others.

This is my seventh trip to Kohler, and for a moment I am not sure why it has taken me so long to sort these things out. Then I remember that I have never before played all four components of the Kohler Quartet in one trip.

To be fair, I am not playing them all this time, for Kohler closed down parts of both River and Meadow Valleys at Blackwolf Run this summer so that golfers could tee it up on the original championship course on which the 1998 US Women's Open was held—and where the 2012 edition of that event was about to be staged. That delightful composite includes holes from both Blackwolf Run tracks and still manages to give a very good sense of what they both have to offer. I have arranged tee times on the Straits and Irish.

The championship course at Blackwolf Run is as good a nature walk as it is a round of golf. I have a hard time not thinking of Winnebagos tapping sugar maples and Chippewas hunting whitetail deer on the property centuries ago as I play my first few holes. Nor can I help marveling at the swathes of purple, yellow, and white wildflowers growing in the deep rough off some fairways. Or delighting in the design of the par-three 6th, with its wildly undulating green rising like a helipad from a creek valley. The best line for the tee shot on a couple of holes demands that I aim at nearby silos, and an old dairy barn serves as a comfort station in the middle of the layout. The maples and birches lining many of the holes are exploding with colors now that it is fall, and their once-green leaves have turned different shades of red, orange, and yellow. And I watch fishermen ply the Sheboygan River (which comes into play on a dozen holes) for salmon, casting flies to shaded pools up and down the waterway.

There is no doubt that I am in Wisconsin when I am at Blackwolf Run. And the drive to Whistling Straits afterward feels like a modern-day hay ride through the Badger State as it takes me past pastures of Holstein cattle and fields tall with corn. But when I step onto the first tee of the Straits course, it seems as if I have been transported to Ireland. The first hole plays down to Lake Michigan, and the next three to the south along bluffs that rise forty feet high. The wind kicks up some whitecaps, yet I can still see some salmon rolling in the waves near the shore. Walking off the 4th tee, after drawing a nice drive into the breeze, I wonder if there is a better start in golf. I know that I have never found four par-threes on any one course that I enjoy as much as these, and I cannot quite believe how disappointed I am when the round is over. Sadly, there isn't even time for an emergency nine.

I go to the Irish the following day. It is the site of my last round on this trip, and the place where I see the light as it relates to golf in Kohler. I fairly float in after that happens on No. 12, feeling downright Gaelic on the 13th, which reminds me of the Dell hole at Lahinch, and on the 14th, where the green is guarded by more than a dozen pot bunkers, and decidedly Midwestern as I finish up the round with other dairy barns and grain silos coming in and out of view.

Revelations, I determine over a pint afterward, are often very good things.

I garner additional enlightenment in the things that my nongolfing wife, Cynthia, and I do off the course while visiting Kohler, which is certainly much more than just a golf resort. It is autumn, and I spend one of my mornings hunting crafty ring-necked pheasants in the River Wildlife preserve that abuts the original Blackwolf Run course Herb Kohler commissioned Pete Dye to build in 1988. I amble through the woods and meadows where the Winnebago and Chippewa Indians once harvested game for their families, my dog flushing the occasional cock bird. I slowly fill my bag, taking plenty of time between shots to admire the stands of old-growth oaks and to savor the sight of silos rising like sentinels above the grain fields in the distance.

I have my limit by noon, and then head for lunch at the restaurant at River Wildlife. A two-story log cabin set in the very woods I have been prowling, it feels like an old-time hunting lodge, with its trophies of ruffed grouse and wild turkey hanging from the walls, displays of antique fishing lures, and prints of sporting scenes, whether a black Labrador retriever bringing in a downed duck or an angler landing a feisty steelhead. And it serves up wonderful fare.

I meet Cynthia there, and she tells me about her morning, which began with a seventy-five-minute massage in the Kohler Waters Spa and was followed by a visit to the Kohler Design Center next door—part museum featuring Kohler products of the past and part showroom with displays of the company's latest offerings. She also took a stroll through the center of the tiny town of Kohler (pop. 1,800), where the quiet streets are lined with leafy trees, Victorian houses featuring wraparound porches, and old-fashioned lamps.

When it is time to order lunch, we both opt for the walleye, the delectable state fish of Wisconsin. Afterward, we head to the Shops at Woodlake, which is located in town and has some twenty different places to browse. We fall hard for place called The Craverie, which is where the Kohler Original Recipe Chocolates are made, buying several boxes as gifts for friends as we also sample a few pieces, to determine whether Oprah Winfrey was right when she put them on one of her O Lists. (After tasting a pyramid-shaped morsel of dark chocolate topped with bits of crystallized ginger, we determine she most certainly was.)

It's late afternoon when we return to the American Club, an elegant inn housed in a three-story Tudor that in the early twentieth century served as a dormitory for Kohler workers and now acts as the centerpiece of the resort. Here we try to work off some of those tasty chocolates on a self-guided tour of the nearby Kohler Gardens. Then it is time for dinner in the Immigrant Room. Also located in the American Club, it is an ace as well. The modest bottle of Anarchy wine that we order is a blend of Syrah, Zinfandel, and Mourvedre grapes, and it is just what we need to accompany the prime, dry-aged strip steaks that we select off the menu, topped as they are with a luscious sauce made with morel mushrooms gathered that day from local woods. I save the last bit of red wine for the cheese course our waiter brings out, with an array of selections all made in Wisconsin. An extraordinarily flavorful piece of twelve-year-old Cheddar, with the calcium lactate crystals that come from aging and make it sharp and slightly crunchy, literally melts in our mouths.

We agree at the end of our meal that we cannot wait to get back here. For the golf, of course. And for everything else.

14

NEBRASKA AND COLORADO

The Sand Hills

I DON'T KNOW IF GEOGRAPHIC VERTIGO IS A COMMON condition, but I suddenly feel as if I have a pretty bad case. Everything about the course I am walking screams Scotland, from the misting skies and biting winds that blow across the treeless landscape to the gaping bunkers and swathes of russet fescue. As I hike up a dune to a tee, I half expect to find a Highlander piping a reel, and maybe even spy the choppy waters of the North Sea.

But what I see instead is an Aerometer windmill and a couple of jackrabbits scampering through fields of black-eyed Susans. And the only sound I hear is that of an Angus heifer mooing between bites of dewy switch grass.

Fact is, I am nowhere near that royal and ancient land. Rather, I am in the sand hills of Nebraska and grappling with the entertaining unlikelihood that this region, so isolated and evocative of the Old American West, is now one of the world's great golf destinations.

It all started with the 1995 opening of the Sand Hills Golf Club outside Mullen (pop. 450). Designed by Ben Crenshaw and Bill Coore, the layout is lauded for its superlative routing and delightful austerity. Then along came Wild Horse Golf Club, a public track created by a pair of architects, Dave Axland and Dan Proctor, who had helped build Sand Hills. Jack Nicklaus added his touch in 2006 at the Dismal River Club, in the form of a dramatic, links-style layout just down the road from Sand Hills that may well be one of the Golden Bear's best. Next to come online was Ballyneal in the northeast corner of Colorado. Not Nebraska, to be sure, but technically part of the sand hills and bestowed with the same geographic attributes. I rank the course that Tom Doak designed there among the top five modern golf layouts in America. The Prairie Club in northern Nebraska opened two tracks in 2010, the Graham Marsh–designed Pines and Tom Lehman's Dunes; soon after that the Jim Engh creation at Awarii Dunes in Kearney, Nebraska (off of Interstate 80), began operations. Then Doak constructed a second course at Dismal River, and it debuted to rave reviews in the summer of 2013.

Now, no one is suggesting that the sand hills are evolving into a second St. Andrews. But the golf there is so good that it is becoming a place to which devout players must make a hajj. Even if the trek can be as arduous as the one to Mecca.

The sand hills make up a 20,000-square-mile island that literally floats on top of a mammoth aquifer. Covered by Cretaceous seas a hundred million years ago, the area was later buried under ice. When those glaciers began to melt, the outwash moved sand into the region, and wind started forming dunes as high as four hundred feet and as long as twenty miles. By 1400 AD, the hills were covered by mineral-rich grasses, creating an environment that centuries later turned out to be perfect for grazing cattle, and—thanks to sandy soil, ample water, and extraordinary elevation changes and land contours—perfect for golf.

People long thought the sand hills, which one pioneer writer described as "frozen waves of prairie ocean," weren't much good for anything. The area remained essentially unpopulated through the Civil War. To be sure, settlers heading west in the nineteenth century occasionally tried to drive their wagons through there, but passage was impossible as their wheels sunk deep into the sand. Almost accidentally, ranchers from the Dakotas discovered the region was good for cattle when they rounded up strays that had disappeared there—and found they were in better shape than when they had left their spreads, due to the shelter the dunes provided and the good grasses. As a result, it began attracting cattle-men, among them Buffalo Bill Cody, who famously hunted bison in the area and then settled near the Dismal River in the 1870s. But the region remained wild, even into the twenty-first century.

It was that cowboy culture that first appealed to Dick Youngscap, a Lincoln, Nebraska, building architect who began visiting the region in the 1980s. He liked the honest friendliness of folks who waved as they passed on the road, whether they knew each other or not, and who happily "neighbored" for fellow ranchers when it was branding time.

There was also the promise that great golf could be nurtured there as well. The trim, white-haired Youngscap had helped develop a Pete Dye course in Lincoln, so he had that designer's eye whenever he took in a landscape. And what he saw outside Mullen convinced him to build the course there, even if that meant building in a part of the state most

Nebraskans have never visited—and most of the country had never heard of.

"It was so obvious golf should be here," he says.

In 1991, Youngscap bought eight thousand acres, and then retained Crenshaw and Coore. After several visits, the architects discovered that the five-hundred-odd acres on which the course was to be built was so golf-rich they mapped out 136 different holes there.

"That's how amazing it was," Coore says. "The land was full of towering dunes and dramatic undulations. It gave us the potential to create something extraordinary, and our biggest concern was not screwing up the incredible opportunity we had been given."

Sand Hills Golf Club created a sensation when it opened. Reviewers praised the way the design worked so naturally with the terrain, and they more or less ignored the fact that it was about a five-hour drive from the nearest major airport in Denver or Omaha. They also lauded the course's charming minimalism, and the way it gave players the same sense of the isolation a lone cowboy might feel when he worked his spread. Youngscap purposely kept accommodations and services modest, too, so they reflected the frontier lifestyle and stark landscape of the region.

But Sand Hills was more than just a great new club. It was also a groundbreaker that ignited a welcome return to site-driven golf course development, which puts a premium on the quality of the land no matter what its location. That approach drove the creation of courses like Pine Valley in the early twentieth century, and it defies the more modern inclination to construct near high-density population centers to ensure heavier usage. The early success of Sand Hills paved the way for Mike Keiser, who was an early member of Sand Hills, to create his fabulous Bandon Dunes retreat several years later and certainly influenced Julian Robertson in his building a pair of spectacular golf courses, Kauri Cliffs and Cape Kidnappers, in faraway (for most people) New Zealand. And it made possible the development of places like Dismal River, Ballyneal, and the Prairie Club.

"Dick was the first," Keiser says. "He's the one who had this pure vision, and he not only imagined it all in the sand hills but also got it done."

There is an awful lot to like about the course at Sand Hill, beginning with the opening hole, a spacious par-five with an elevated tee that overlooks a very welcoming fairway some 65 yards wide. It is a wonderful way to start a game, and I become even more enthralled by the layout when I get to the short par-fours at Nos. 7 and 8. One requires a draw off the tee, and the other a fade. One plays to an elevated green, and the other to a putting surface set in a natural amphitheater, testing a golfer's skills as it also tickles his fancy. There are also holes like the 17th, a 150-yard par-three to a green set on a dune and surrounded by bunkers filled with sand as fine as sugar.

The angles of the tee shots throughout the round enchant me, and the approaches, whether wedges or hybrids or clubs in between, are as fun as they are challenging. I cannot help but think at times of a friend back home who likes to remind me to enjoy each golf shot I make. I make a point of doing that every time I play Sand Hills, reveling in the visuals of a wild and wooly place that seems so far removed from civilization, and with a design that has me begging for more.

The situation at Dismal River, which is named after the spring-fed river that was the site of a battle led by Buffalo Bill in the Indian Wars and is a little more than ten miles away from Sand Hills, is not dissimilar. Nicklaus asserts that he found the land there just as full of design options; he saw a golf hole in every direction he looked. Both are links-style designs that required little earth moving, and they each feature the vast blowout bunkers, steep knolls, and hidden glens so characteristic of this locus.

Still, there are differences, especially on the greens, which are more severe at Dismal River. The elevation changes feel more drastic there, too, and the accommodations are a little less spartan. And now, Dismal River has a second layout. Designed by Doak, it gives this semiprivate retreat one of the best one-two punches in golf, and I like how Doak has routed the back nine of this course along the Dismal River and at the foot of a two-hundred-yard bluff. The course is a keeper, and it is hard for anyone walking that ground not to imagine buffaloes rumbling by—and Indian hunters chasing after them.

Ballyneal is located in the chop hills outside the farming town of Holyoke in northeast Colorado, roughly a two-and-a-half-hour drive from Denver, and Doak employed the same minimalist approach here, with brilliant results. Holes wind smartly in and around the dunes, demanding that players hit every club in their bag—and every type of shot they know. Each one is memorable, but none more so than the par-five 4th, where an elevated tee gives players a chance to crush one of the most fun drives in golf, as well as to take in one of the game's greatest views, the rugged hills stretching out for miles in all directions.

As a longtime wing shooter, I also like how Ballyneal offers superlative upland bird hunting in nearby grain fields that are full of wild ringed-neck pheasants. The action for those elegant fliers can be fast and furious in the fall.

The two tracks at the Prairie Club, which is situated outside the town of Valentine, Nebraska, near the South Dakota border, provide very different feels of golf in the sand hills. The Pines runs through woods along the Snake River Valley and, as a result, feels like a modern Pine Valley. As for the Dunes, it is much more a traditional links, with massive fairways and greens, testy undulations, and almost constant winds blowing across land that has plenty of character but feels less dramatic than at Sand Hills or Dismal River.

The Prairie Club is also home to what is called the Horse Course. Designed by Gil Hanse and Geoff Shackleford, the layout comprises ten holes, none of which are longer than 115 yards. The idea is to play it as if you were playing a game of H-O-R-S-E in basketball, with the golfer who wins a hole determining the place from which the tee shots are hit on the next. It is a terrific end-of-day diversion, especially with a cold pint of ale in hand.

Walking to the 5th tee on the Dunes during one of my rounds there, I see the remains of the foundation of a nineteenth-century homestead as well as an old wagon wheel and plow half buried in brush. Later, my caddie tells me that some of the roads running through the club were once wagon trails. As I walk to my next shot, I take a moment to appreciate yet again the delightful combination of old-time golf and the Old West—and to take note of how well it all works, no matter how geographically confusing it may sometimes be.

Certainly, the Sand Hills Golf Club looms large in this region, and understandably so. Ditto the Prairie Club and Dismal River, both of which attract a lot of attention in the greater golf world. Ballyneal, too. Their collective prominence makes it easy to overlook another pair of gems in the area.

One of those is the Wild Horse Golf Club in Gothenberg, Nebraska, a former stop on the Pony Express just off Interstate 80. Opened in 1999, Wild Horse was designed by Dave Axland and Dan Proctor, both of whom helped build Sand Hills. The land has neither the remoteness nor topographical diversity of that great track, but the wind blows frequently, the soil is sandy, and the undulations sinister and subtle.

Some golfers affectionately call Wild Horse "Sand Hills Lite." Shot placement is critical, and trouble awaits anyone who put his ball into the ankle-high prairie grass that lines most landing areas. The rugged bunkers, some of which lie in the middle of fairways, give the layout a natural look and ethos, and they also do a superb job of protecting par.

Houses have been constructed around parts of the Wild Horse course, and I frequently hear freight train whistles during a round. It reminds me of how much closer I am to the civilized world than at Sand Hills or Dismal River. But the bleached-out cow skulls serving as 150-yard markers remind me that I am still very much in ranch country.

Down the highway in Kearney is Awarii Dunes. Named for the Pawnee word meaning "windblown," it feels an awful lot like Wild Horse: for its proximity to the interstate, for the houses that rise along some of its borders and the nearby fields of corn and soybeans, and for its minimalist design. Architect Jim Engh describes Awarii as his homage to Ireland, and while it has neither the drama of those more dunesy layouts nor vistas of wave-pocked seas, it compels golfers to employ more of a ground game. The course has an out-in-front-of-you design with wonderful holes that were deftly sculpted from the land, especially the stretch from Nos. 12 to 15 that includes three par-threes and a pair of five-pars.

Engh made excellent use of what he found at Awarii, and Axland and Proctor did the same at Wild Horse. They may not be as drop-dead spectacular as the better-known layouts in the sand hills. But they, too, are worth a visit—and give golfers even more reason to spend more than a few days in this special part of the world.

15

NOVA SCOTIA AND PRINCE EDWARD ISLAND

Northern Links

CABOT LINKS IS ONLY ONE GOLF COURSE, MIND YOU. But this stunning seaside design on the western shores of Cape Breton has singlehandedly transformed what was a pretty good golf destination into one of the finest in North America. The recent creation of a second, equally enticing track there, Cabot Cliffs, has elevated that status even higher, as has the recent revamping of Highland Links, the historic Stanley Thompson layout about ninety minutes up the road. Throw in the nearby track at Bell Bay in Baddeck, and you have a very formidable foursome of places to play in Nova Scotia. And when you combine those retreats with some of the courses on neighboring Prince Edward Island, you end up with an embarrassment of golfing riches—and some very compelling reasons to travel to those parts with your sticks. Especially when you also consider the low-key, pastoral ethos of those provinces and their natural beauty.

O Canada!

Opened in 2012, Cabot Links is named after the Italian explorer Giovanni Caboto, the first European adventurer to come to North America (and who the English-speaking world long ago took to calling John Cabot). It is located in Inverness, the quiet Cape Breton fishing and mining village where some road signs are still in Gaelic and Celtic music is often played in local bars. The names of many people and places in this area have Old World roots, like Macpherson and Macdonald, which seems appropriate when you consider that Nova Scotia translates into "New Scotland." So does the increasing presence of golf in a place named after the game's ancestral home.

The force behind Cabot Links is Toronto entrepreneur Ben Cowan-Dewar. He put together the deal for the two hundred acres on which the course is laid out, a complicated process that involved eleven different parcels, one of which included an old coal mine locals had worked for years. Cowan-Dewar was also responsible for bringing in Mike Keiser as a partner, the man who developed the superb Bandon Dunes property on the Oregon coast, and hiring the notable Canadian architect Rod Whitman to handle the course design.

For Cowan-Dewar, creating Cabot Links was in many ways the culmination of a life that has been closely connected to golf. As a five-year-old, he began sketching his own designs of golf holes on pieces of paper. Soon, he was thinking of becoming a course architect, and he was only ten when he and his stockbroker father built an actual hole on their farm outside Toronto. One year later, Cowan-Dewar began organizing golf trips in and out of Canada for family members.

So it is really not that surprising that Cowan-Dewar became deeply immersed in the royal and ancient game as an adult. As the head of a tour business, as one of the fellows running Golf Club Atlas, the wildly popular website and forum dedicated to golf course architecture, and as the co-owner and founder of Cabot Links.

Cowan-Dewar first visited the Cabot Links property in December 2004, when he was living in Toronto and working in the financial services industry. He was so enthralled with the land's potential that he returned a few weeks later with Whitman, who had learned about golf course construction and design while working for the great Pete Dye. Cowan-Dewar was not the first person to have considered the possibilities of building a course there, as designers as wide ranging as Jack Nicklaus and Greg Norman had previously checked it out. But the Ontario native was the only one who got beyond swooning over the dazzling property by acquiring it in 2007 and then proceeding with its development. Course construction began a year later, with Whitman laying out a links-style track between the shore and a two-lane roadway called the Cabot Trail that cuts through Inverness (pop. 1,800).

I relished my first rounds at Cabot Links, with the wind blowing off the Gulf of St. Lawrence and shots running firm and fast on fescue fairways and greens. And my affection has only grown in subsequent visits. I love how the course not only harkens back to the Scottish links of yore but also channels Bandon, with its somewhat hard-to-reach locale and celebration of golf played and enjoyed in the most traditional ways. There are no swathes of gorse, per se. But the pockets of wispy rough; small, scruffy pines; and gnarly scrubs and bushes penalize players for errant shots in much the same way they enhance the layout's look and feel. The connection to the traditional game is further strengthened by the sight of Wolf Island just offshore, looming beyond the layout like the Ailsa Craig at Turnberry.

As for the golf holes themselves, I find it hard to pick a favorite. The second hole is a testy five-par running southwest, where you have to carry a gaping chasm to get to the green if you play down the right side, while No. 5 is an inspired rendition of the classic Biarritz Charles, Blair Macdonald, and Seth Raynor built on so many of their courses, playing 225 yards most days to a green bisected by a deep swale. The 8th and 9th holes are routed along a tidal pond that boasts a small lobster boat dock. And the 14th is Whitman's homage to the iconic 7th at Pebble Beach, a downhill three-par that measures a mere 102 yards from the tips, usually requiring a very deft short iron to a green perched right on the water.

Once Cabot Links came online, Cowan-Dewar and Keiser commissioned Bill Coore and Ben Crenshaw to build Cabot Cliffs on a dramatic site outside Inverness that also overlooks the gulf. It gives the developers the sort of spectacular twosome that keeps visitors happily engaged there for several days at a time, playing one round after another and never wanting to leave.

Players should be just as enthralled with Highland Links. Stanley Thompson routed this gem on the eastern edge of the Cape Breton Highlands National Park in the late 1930s, constructing the first few holes hard on the Atlantic Ocean. Then, the track turns inland, feeling as much like a nature hike as a round of golf. The first time I teed it there, I half expected to find Acadian trappers paddling a birch bark canoe down the Clyburn River as it cut through that portion of the course, so virginal and timeless it all seemed.

Almost due south, just outside the modest town of Baddeck, is a newer Cape Breton layout that turns some very learned golfing heads as well—Bell Bay. The name Bell comes from inventor Alexander Graham Bell, who lived and worked on his summer estate just across a bay from the course Canadian Thomas McBroom designed in the late 1990s. Golfers catch glimpses of Bell's old workshop from the second fairway as well as the 18th tee—and gaze across the vast Bras d'Or, which is Cape Breton's inland sea, and the majestic boats that cut across it. Some holes duck over hills and into hollows, forcing players to hit approach shots over gorges and ravines—and allowing them to experience the woods there as much as the water.

Nova Scotia's neighbor to the west, Prince Edward Island (PEI), has a number of courses worth playing. One of the best is the Links at Crowsbush, another McBroom design with several holes routed by a vast beach and in and around stands of birches and firs. Just as good is Dundarave, created by American architects Mike Hurdzan and Dana Fry. It gives new meaning to the term "parklands" course because Dundarave truly feels as if you are playing in a park. A national park, that is, of almost indescribable beauty. I am so energized after I stripe my tee shot on the par-four 8th, a short, well-bunkered dogleg with water all the way down the left side and behind the green, that I let out a whoop so loud that a clam digger working a nearby sand bar looks up in wonder.

To be fair, no one is going to be holding a major championship on those two layouts, and they each have a hole or two that could stand some tweaking. But generally speaking, the courses are as fun as they are visually compelling. And they project a feel as comforting as PEI itself. It is the sort of place where churches still hold weekly haddock fries and lobster pots are stacked on lawns. Hay, barley, and corn flourish in fertile fields of brick-red soil, as do several varieties of potatoes, the province's most famous and delectable agricultural export. Vegetable stands abound, lining many of the often-empty island roads and existing entirely on the honor system.

They call PEI the gentle island, and Nova Scotia boasts a similar aura, one that is reminiscent of kinder, perhaps better times. "I wish I had a dollar for everyone who ever told me it reminds him of his hometown fifty years ago," a local golfer says after a round, as we pick through a bowl of tasty Prince Edward Island mussels, which are served complimentary at many 19th holes. "People love it here for that."

That is certainly part of what makes me like the Maritimes so much—the vast beaches, roiling seas, and delectable seafood, too. And, of course, the golf.

16

BANFF AND JASPER
Rocky Mountain Highs

THERE MAY NOT BE A BETTER PLACE IN THE WORLD TO hike than the Canadian Rockies.

That's what I thought as I strode down a trail in Jasper National Park, the largest in the country and some 4,300 square miles in size. The morning sun cast soft light across the granite crags that loomed all around as it also illuminated the snow that capped some of the rocky peaks and the ice fields that blanketed the flatter areas on high. Stands of conifers swept across verdant valleys and up steel-gray mountainsides, and roiling rivers the color of larimar cut through grassy meadows. The air was crisp, even though it was midsummer, and smelled faintly of wood burning in the fireplaces of nearby cabins.

I felt the same way a couple of days later as I visited Banff National Park, just to the south. Established in 1885, it is a bit smaller than Jasper, at roughly 2,500 square miles but no less scenic, which I realized as soon as I walked by the almost vertical face of Mount Rundle and admired the avalanche chutes that ran down it like rocky tentacles.

Normally, I tote a rucksack when I wander through woods and along waters such as these. But I had a golf bag slung over my shoulder instead, for these hills and dales also happen to be home to some of the best golf in North America.

The rugged scenery and splendid isolation set these places apart as golf destinations, each as visually gorgeous and evocative as an Ansel Adams photograph. So does the sensation of being in the wild, and of teeing it up on courses where most mornings the sand in the bunkers are marred by big game tracks, and a common query among regular players at the start of each round is not the obligatory, "What's your handicap?" but rather, "Have you seen any bears recently?"

But the layouts are what make these retreats truly great. Especially the two I played here, Banff Springs Golf Club and Jasper Park Lodge Golf Club, both of which are gems laid out nearly a century ago by the brilliant Canadian architect Stanley Thompson.

A protégé of Harry S. Colt and a one-time caddie who was one of nine children born to Scottish immigrant parents, Thompson was a first-rate golfer who came to be known as the Toronto Terror for a lifestyle that was as flamboyant as many of his course designs. As a designer, he believed in preserving the natural lay and flow of the land on which he worked, and he was as prolific as he was good, designing or remodeling 145 layouts in his lifetime and earning a well-deserved reputation as one of the game's greatest architects.

Jasper was the first course I played, and it is not only one of Thompson's best but also one of Canada's finest. I appreciated the high quality of the layout as soon as I stepped to the first tee, on which a traditional Indian totem pole stood, and considered the uphill par-four that requires a well-placed drive just short of a fairway bunker on the right and then an accurate long iron to a spacious green with lots of subtle breaks. And things only got better from there. Snow-covered mountains rising behind the well-bunkered green on the par-five 2nd made that approach shot as scenic as it was challenging, and I lingered over it so long that I worried about getting called for slow play by my partners. The same thing happened when I arrived at the tee for the 231-yard par-three 9th, which Thompson named Cleopatra in part for the dramatic summit of Pyramid Mountain soaring behind the long, narrow green but also for the bumps and mounds he built before it to resemble, *ahem,* the rather buxom body of the one-time Queen of Egypt.

Thompson fancied elevated tees and gaping bunkers that boast flashes and fingerlings and were sometimes shaped to look like the crags climbing into the sky beyond them. He also liked to use those as aiming points for tee shots, for he relished the great views Jasper offered and would spend hours walking the property as he contemplated the course he was routing there, often nipping from a flask of gin along the way. As much as he loved the mountains, though, he was sure to make good use of the expansive lake on which Jasper Lodge, which opened in 1915, is built, and around which a series of small log cabins are arrayed. The drive off the scenic 14th tee requires a tight draw over the waters of Lac Beauvert to a canted fairway that doglegs to the left, and the lake also comes into play on Nos. 15 and 16.

Jasper was Thompson's maiden architectural triumph, and he found himself much in demand after it opened in 1925. One of the first gigs he took after that was to lay out a golf course at the Banff Spring National Park a few hours' drive due south on Highway 93. Built by laborers on Depression-era work projects, the road winds between hoary mountain peaks and along lush meadows, dense fir forests,

and rivers roiling from snowmelt. I damn near drove off
the asphalt as I motored through the Columbia Ice Field,
so enthralled was I by the thick stretches of ice still covering
the ground. I almost wrecked again a few miles later when I
came around a corner to find a herd of mountain goats cross-
ing the highway. Whiter than the ice in the fields I had just
passed and the snow that blanketed some of the hills, they
were seemingly unconcerned with human intrusion, nibbling
quietly on shoots of grass on either side of the thoroughfare.

In many ways, the jobs at Jasper and Banff were quite
similar, given that Thompson was working with wild, open land
that possessed great character, extraordinary vistas, and almost
endless design possibilities. The terrain at Banff was a little flatter than what Thompson had at Jasper, and he had to bring
in loads of topsoil and sand to complete his work there. The
designer also did a fair amount of blasting, and by the time
work on the Banff track was done, in 1929, it had cost $1 mil-
lion, a record for golf course construction at that time.

As expensive as that may have seemed, however, it must
fairly be regarded as money well spent, for Banff Springs is
a revelation. Every tee box feels like a lookout point, beginning with the par-four 1st, and continuing through Nos. 2, 3,
and 4, all of which are cut in the shadow of Mount Rundle, so
close at times that a golfer might feel as if it could fall down
right on top of him. Teeing off on the par-three 4th, which
is known as the Devil's Cauldron, I felt as if I was hitting into
the mountain itself, and the sheer delight of Thompson's
design only grows through the round. I had to hit draws and
fades off the tees, and I needed to run up some approach
shots and land others on the greens, all of which are full of
charm and guile. The Bow River running along Nos. 8–14
provided pleasing midround visuals, and while the ascent
to the aerie-like 15th tee left me gasping for breath, I happily did it again that afternoon for the simple joy of crushing

another drive from that perch—and watching my golf ball hang lazily in the cool Canadian air before falling to the fairway 250 yards away.

As for the lodge at Banff, it is an imposing, castle-like structure made of Rundle stone and roofed with thick slate shingles. Big, regal, and imposing, it comes into view for golfers on the first few holes of the back nine and presents them with a stunning backdrop as they play in.

It is hard to beat the walk in these two parks. Or the golf.

17

PINEHURST
America's St. Andrews

As an ardent fan of Bobby Jones, I was pretty much down with anything the golfing great was quoted as saying. Until, that is, I made my first trip some years ago to the Carolina Sand Hills.

That was when I learned that he had once called Pinehurst "the St. Andrews of United States golf." Frankly, I did not get the analogy. Pinehurst is not built on linksland, nor located by the sea. As its name suggests, loblolly and longleaf pines abound here, and that is not the sort of flora one associates with the Home of Golf. I found nary a swathe of gorse during that maiden journey to Pinehurst, nor does anyone speak in a Scottish brogue. The climate was much more temperate in this Southern retreat, and I learned that the drink of choice at many postround watering holes was bourbon, not single malt whisky.

All of which made me wonder what Bobby Jones was thinking of when he uttered those words.

But I went back to Pinehurst a few more times after that initial voyage, and those visits helped me understand just what the man meant.

Located in central North Carolina, about seventy-five miles from the state capital of Raleigh, Pinehurst was established in the late 1800s by James Walker Tufts, a Boston philanthropist and soda fountain magnate. After purchasing some 5,800 acres, he set out to create a New England–style hamlet in what had once been a vibrant logging area and make it a middle-class health retreat for northerners. To that end, Tufts engaged the noted landscape architect Frederick Law Olmstead, who had designed New York City's Central Park, to create a master plan for the property. Streets, sewers, and water systems were constructed, as well as a general store, a dairy, and a boarding house. Then Tufts opened the Holly Inn, in December 1895, and after that the Carolina Hotel. In time, the resort began to offer its guests riding, lawn bowling, tennis, and archery among other activities. Shooting also evolved as a popular pastime, and for a spell, the person in charge of the Pinehurst Gun Club was Annie Oakley, the famed female sharpshooter who was the star of Buffalo Bill's Wild West show.

But it was golf that became the favorite recreation at Pinehurst. In the very early days of the resort, guests took to banging *gutta perchas* in and around neighboring pastures. But the farmers did not like how their livestock was disturbed by such sporting nonsense, and they complained vehemently to Tufts. So, in 1898, he built a rudimentary 9-hole golf course for his clientele. A year later, he added a second nine, and the first 18-hole track became known simply as Pinehurst No. 1, its square greens made of oiled sand. Notables such as industrialist John D. Rockefeller and US president William McKinley came to play; Englishman Harry Vardon even conducted a series of golf demonstrations there. But what really gave the royal and ancient game a boost there was the hiring in 1900 of a young Scottish golf professional named Donald Ross to oversee all golf operations.

Born and raised in Dornoch, Scotland, Ross showed promise as a golfer as a young man, and also great proficiency as a carpenter. So he went to St. Andrews to apprentice as a club maker to Old Tom Morris. Upon Ross's return to Dornoch, he became the first professional and greenskeeper of the golf club there. Then, in 1899, he emigrated to the United States, arriving in the Commonwealth of Massachusetts with only $7 in his pocket and no job. He soon found work at the Oakley Country Club in Watertown, Massachusetts, where one of the members happened to be James Tufts. Yes, the very same man who was building Pinehurst, and who would hire Ross to come work for his new resort.

One of the first things Ross did upon his arrival at Pinehurst was redesign the No. 1 course. Then in 1907, he laid out his first 18-holer, a championship track dubbed No. 2. It, too, featured sand greens, and Ross produced a course with deft bunkering, minimal rough, and interesting angles on drives and approach shots. In later years, Ross, who was a strong enough player to have finished fifth in the 1903 US Open and eighth in the 1910 Open Championship, constructed two more courses at Pinehurst, Nos. 3 and 4, and he continued to tweak those tracks on an almost annual basis until his death in 1948. During his time in the United States, much of which was spent living in a cottage off the third hole of No. 2, the Scotsman would be credited with the design of some four hundred golf courses around the country. But he would always be most closely associated with those tracks in Pinehurst, especially the one known as No. 2.

It wasn't long before Pinehurst No. 2 became one of the most celebrated layouts in the land, a hallowed place for resort guests and also a popular tournament venue for professionals and amateurs. The course was the site for nearly five decades of the esteemed North and South Open and also the North and South Amateur Golf Championships, which exist to this day. Those drew some of the best golfers in the country to Pinehurst, and Bobby Jones, Gene Sarazen, Byron Nelson, Glenna Collett Vare, and Babe Zaharias all competed there. Pinehurst No. 2 was also the host of the 1936 PGA Championship, won by Denny Shute, as well as the 1951 Ryder Cup matches, when an American team captained by Sam Snead and including Ben Hogan, Jackie Burke, and Jimmy Demaret prevailed.

The USGA staged the 1962 US Amateur at Pinehurst, and it was also the site of the 1991 and 1992 PGA Tour Championships. Then, in 1999, the Home of Golf in America got its first US Open, and it was a stirring competition, with the late Payne Stewart draining a fifteen-foot putt for par on the 18th hole for one of the most dramatic wins in tournament history. Stewart celebrated his victory with a one-legged fist pump, a move that has been immortalized in a statue of the golfing great behind the 18th green at No. 2.

Six years later, Michael Campbell of New Zealand beat Tiger Woods by two strokes to capture the second US Open ever held at Pinehurst, and soon after that, the USGA decided to put on both the Men's and Women's Opens at No. 2, in the summer of 2014.

A lot has changed at Pinehurst in the years since the days of Donald Ross. The resort now has a total of eight golf courses, with new designs created in the modern era by Rees Jones (No. 7), Tom Fazio (Nos. 6 and 8), and Ellis Maples, a protégé of Ross's who designed No. 5 in the early 1960s. There have also been plenty of nips and tucks of the original tracks, including Fazio's revamping of No. 4 and the stellar renovation of No. 2 that Ben Crenshaw and Bill Coore completed in 2011. Their mandate was to return the course to its more natural condition of the 1940s and 1950s, and they did that by stripping out acres of Bermuda grass rough and reintroducing hardpan and native wiregrasses.

But all that growth has done nothing to alter Pinehurst's character as a quaint and quiet spot, with a village population of roughly thirteen thousand. And golf remains the central form of recreation there as well as the primary topic of conversation among residents and visitors alike, thanks not only to those resort courses but also to the roughly three dozen tracks that have been built within easy access of town over the years.

After getting to know Pinehurst a bit better, it was easier to discern the many similarities between the two Homes of Golf. They have comparable populations. They both exude a sort of small-town charm. And they offer oodles of golf, with there now being more than forty courses within a fifteen-mile radius of Pinehurst. As is the case in Auld Grey Toon, many of those tracks are open to the public and in very close proximity, so golfers can quickly hop from one to another. In addition, the two retreats have a cluster of courses at their epicenter, with the five layouts on the links of St. Andrews and an equal number within an easy walk of the Carolina Hotel at the Pinehurst Resort, in the form of Nos. 1, 2, 3, 4, and 5. There also are similarities in terrain, as the locales each have sand-based soil that is perfectly suited for golf and ground with lots of contours and character.

I came to realize that golf is widely spoken—and adored—in the two spots. No matter what restaurant we entered in Pinehurst, no matter what bar we bellied up to, the conversation—among ourselves and all around us—centered on the royal and ancient game. Just like in St.

Andrews. And golf showed its presence in Pinehurst in many other ways. One night, I dined with friends at the Pine Crest Inn, which Donald Ross owned from 1921 until his death in 1948. While we ate in the dining room, patrons in the lounge abutting that area were trying their hands at a long-time Pinehurst tradition, which involves chipping golf balls through a hole in a board situated in a fireplace. On several occasions during our meal, balls suddenly came bouncing into the dining room, the result of errant bits of wedge play, with the people responsible for the misses scrambling in behind them and then disappearing back into the bar.

Much as the Old Course is the biggest draw in St. Andrews, Pinehurst No. 2 is where everyone wants to tee it here. Understandably so. But the other tracks of the Pinehurst resort are worth checking out. And so are places like the Dormie Club, a nearby private retreat that like many of its ilk in these more trying economic times is opening itself in a variety of ways to outside play. Laid out by Coore and Crenshaw, it offers everything and anything a golfer could want. Short par-fours? There is one on each side here, each a tick under 300 yards and crafted in fair and insightful ways. You like them longer? No problem, for there is the 472-yard par-four on the front side, and a 465-yarder on the back. Looking for a devilish par-three? Then you will love the 108-yarder here that plays to a testy, well-bunkered green.

You don't need to be a member to get on another pair of must-plays, the excellent Donald Ross layouts at the Pine Needles and Mid Pines resorts, and legend has it that the architect long considered Pine Needles his favorite to play. The two Tom Fazio golf courses at the Forest Creek Country Club are on most every top ten list of layouts to visit in North Carolina, as are the tracks at the Country Club of North Carolina, one of which (Dogwood) was where Hal Sutton won the 1980 US Amateur. Another hidden gem is the Southern

Pines Golf Club, which is known to locals as the Elks Club, because that is who owns it. It, too, is a Donald Ross design, and while the conditioning is not always up to par, the routing and bunkering are top shelf.

During my most recent trip to Pinehurst, I played No. 4 for the first time, which designer Tom Fazio has described as his homage to Ross. Fazio put 180 pot bunkers on this layout, and they present real problems if your game is the least bit off. It is a distinctly Pinehurst track, with its stands of loblollies, gnarly waste areas, and upside-down saucer-shaped greens that can make it exceedingly difficult at times to hold approach shots. The course is also ringed by roads and within sight of a couple of the other Pinehurst tracks, which were two more things that reminded me of St. Andrews, and what Bobby Jones said about this being its US equivalent.

How could I have ever doubted him?

18

NEW YORK
Across the Empire State

THE GOLFING UNIVERSE IN THE EMPIRE STATE HAS LONG revolved around New York City and suburban counties in neighboring Westchester County and on Long Island. And that's largely because most of the best courses in the state are located there. Places like Garden City and Quaker Ridge as well as Maidstone and the National Golf Links of America. The quality of those tracks and the histories of the clubs formed around them are big reasons why golfers hold those spots in such esteem and do whatever they can to play them. It is also what compels the top golf associations to host so many major championships there. To be sure, they venture upstate on occasion, to places like Oak Hill Golf Club in Rochester, which is hosting the PGA in summer 2015. But as a rule, the USGA and PGA favor places much closer to the Big Apple when they decide to come to New York. Such as Winged Foot and Shinnecock Hills.

As understandable and rational as those impulses may be, they sometimes obscure the fact that there is plenty of very strong golf in other realms of New York. What may make that reality even more appealing to the peripatetic player is that unlike metropolitan New York, the vast majority of courses upstate are public and open to any and all comers.

Start with the Turning Stone Resort and Casino, owned by the Oneida Indian Nation and situated just east of Syracuse in the town of Verona. It boasts an impressive trio of tracks, one designed by Tom Fazio and the other two by Robert Trent Jones II and Rick Smith. They are as challenging for recreational golfers as they are well conditioned and fun to play. Way to the west, near the shores of Lake Erie and not far from the Pennsylvania border, is the Chautauqua Institution, a nationally renowned summer community devoted to the pleasures of learning about art, education, religion, and politics—and also enjoying a bit of recreation. Thankfully, golf is among the more popular diversions there, and the institution has two layouts, the Hill and the Lake. While both are pleasing places to play, the Donald Ross–designed Lake Course stands out, as much for its serene setting and subtle routing as for a rich history that includes Amelia Earhart once landing a plane on the 17th fairway and Gene Sarazen carding an albatross on the 10th (eventually leading members to dub the club bar Double Eagle). Back toward Albany are the charming village of Cooperstown and the Leatherstocking Golf Club, named for an occurring character in the books penned by native son James Fenimore Cooper and designed by one of the game's architectural greats, Devereux Emmet.

Golf alone is good enough reason to head to these parts. But travelers can find so much more along the way. I took a respite from my rounds when I drove through the Finger Lakes, a mostly rural region comprising farms, vineyards, small towns, and vacation homes, and embarked on a number of craft beer and wine tastings and sampled first-rate food served in restaurants with a strong farm-to-table ethic. I also enjoyed museum tours in Cooperstown that touched on everything from nineteenth-century farm life and Native American art to Major League Baseball. There's gaming, to be sure, in Turning Stone, and auto racing in Watkins Glen, as well as hikes through wooded hills and boating on placid waters. Productions of the Glimmerglass Opera in Cooperstown are musical triumphs, as are the pieces that the remarkably versatile Chautauqua Symphony plays so deftly on sultry summer nights. Morning lectures in that town's five-thousand-seat amphitheater cover topics on art and politics as well as sociology and science, and so do afternoon discussions in the open-air Hall of Philosophy.

As someone who grew up close to New York City, and who was raised to believe that the world truly turns around that grand metropolis, spending time upstate was a happy revelation. The golf was great there. But that wasn't all.

Generally speaking, I am not a gambler. At least off the golf course (as I must confess to finding that a modest Nassau always makes a round a little more interesting). So the idea of going to a casino has little or no appeal. I will, however, always take to the road for good golf, and in the end, that is what made my trip to the Turning Stone Resort, which opened in 1993, so compelling.

I didn't play one hand of blackjack in the massive gaming complex during my stay there, which boasts more than 120,000 square feet of space dedicated to every conceivable form of gambling. Nor did I put even one quarter in a slot machine. But I did tee it up on each of Turning Stone's three golf courses—Atunyote, Shenendoah, and Kaluhyat—and they may very well make this 3,400-acre retreat in the heart of the Oneida Nation, not far from the city of Syracuse, the best golf destination in the state.

As for the gaming, I can only judge by what I saw on a couple of quick swings through the casino. Which was a place bustling with activity at all hours of the day and night, not only at the poker and craps tables or at the more than twenty-two hundred gaming machines but also in the different restaurants serving everything from Brazilian-style steaks and Asian fusion food to a five-thousand-seat event center that regularly hosts top music and comedy acts. And what that told me is that if you are the sort who is just as inclined to let a few dollars ride in roulette as you are to seek out a well-designed golf course, then this truly is the place for you.

As for me, the golf was all I needed.

My favorite Turning Stone track was Shenendoah, designed by Rick Smith and named after the heroic Oneida tribal chief who sided with the colonials in the Revolutionary War. The course was the first of the three 18-holers to open at the resort, in the year 2000, and it has something of a heath-lands feel, with wide fairways that dip, rise, and bend with the many changes of elevation. Stands of field grass stretch along the holes, their pale green colors flecked with yellow and white wildflowers. Smith protects par quite ably with well-positioned bunkers, and when I played the par-72 course from the blue tees that measure roughly 6,600 yards, I quite happily found myself hitting a variety of approaches. Sometimes it was a hybrid to an elevated green, and other times a short iron to a tucked pin. Sections of wetlands give the land an even wilder feel, and the five sets of tees make it playable for golfers of all abilities.

I also liked the Trent Jones track called Kaluhyat, which means "other side of the sky" in the Oneida language, almost as much. Built in 2003, it, too, has very dramatic contours and boasts several plateaus that not only offer sweeping views but also give great character to the holes. Again, the mix of shots and looks is strong, and the five lakes provide strong visuals.

Especially on the par-five 13th, a dogleg right dubbed Big Water, and also No. 7, known as Meadow Spirit and demanding a draw off the tee.

Tom Fazio laid out his Atunyote course in 2004 on a parcel of land some two miles from the resort with a deadwood marsh, lots of rock formations, and several lakes, streams, and waterfalls. It is the longest of the three Turning Stone tracks, at 7,482 yards, and was built to host a PGA Tour event. To that end, Atunyote, which is the Oneida word for "eagle," is the place where the PGA Tour held its Turning Stone Resort Championship for three years, and its BC Open once, in 2006. The course was also the site that same year of the PGA Professional National Championship and is where Notah Begay has hosted his NB3 Foundation Challenge since 2008. I found the track to be a superb test and good fun to walk, with deep, flat-bottomed bunkers featuring steep, well-defined slopes that are very reminiscent of Augusta National. As scenic as the property is, though, it is not quite as interesting as the land at Kaluhyat or Shenendoah. But when combined with the other two courses, it makes playing golf at Turning Stone anything but a gamble.

If Turning Stone is a place where golfers also try to accumulate monetary wealth, at the Indian casino's slot machines and gaming tables, then the western New York State village of Chautauqua is for those looking to amass capital of the intellectual variety—from the multitude of lectures and discussions that are organized on its bucolic grounds and the concerts and plays that are staged in its theaters. And through the dozens of classes that are taught each day on wide-ranging subjects, classes such as Ancient Greece, Ballroom Dancing, and Knitting with Dog Hair.

Located on the shores of a lake by that same name, Chautauqua describes itself as a place for active thinkers, and the first thing that most residents and visitors seem to ask themselves when they wake is: What do I want to learn today? Apparently, I want to learn a lot, for I am running myself ragged, attending morning talks by South Asian diplomats about the state of affairs in Pakistan and evening performances by the community's sterling symphony orchestra, including one that began with an overture written decades ago by occasional Chautauqua visitor George Gershwin. There are cooking classes, too, and meetings of the Chautauqua Literary and Scientific Circle, founded in 1878 and regarded as the oldest, continually operating book club in America. As I climb into bed at night, I find myself thoroughly yet ecstatically exhausted by the knowledge I am absorbing. Or at the very least trying to.

Truth be told, I am also spent by all the golf I am playing at the Chautauqua Golf Club, which has two courses, including a fine Donald Ross design. But I do not feel the least bit guilty about heading out to the links so often. Folks here have long believed that it is as important to take care of the body as it is the mind. And I am doing my level best to tend to both.

Chautauqua is the name of the town where the Chautauqua Institution operates for nine weeks each summer. Founded by Methodists in 1874, it originally was a training camp for Sunday School teachers. And while its religious roots remain strong, with worship services held for multiple denominations through the session, the institution has also evolved into an intellectual retreat. Leading thinkers from around the world come to Chautauqua to lecture, perform, or create. Susan B. Anthony spoke for women's suffrage in its amphitheater in 1892, for example, and Franklin Delano Roosevelt gave his "I Hate War" speech from the same dais, in 1936. Margaret Mead visited, too, and Thurgood Marshall. President Bill Clinton spent a week in Chautauqua in 1996, preparing for his debate with candidate Bob Dole.

That made Clinton the tenth US president to venture here. Duke Ellington and Willie Nelson have played concerts on the grounds, and authors like Kurt Vonnegut have spoken. Former US senator Sam Nunn recently came to Chautauqua to share his thoughts on nuclear disarmament, while NFL commissioner Roger Goodell discussed the league that he runs, and its present, past, and future.

The opportunities to listen to and watch such interesting men and women make Chautauqua a very special retreat. So does a small-town ethos that harkens back to another time. Set on just over 225 acres, the institution is a community in the truest sense of the word, and the sort of town that only seems to exist these days in Norman Rockwell paintings. Some twelve hundred gingerbread-style cottages line the quiet, maple-shaded streets. Kids pedal bicycles from place to place, and adults gather on porches to visit with friends and family. TVs are rarely on, doors only occasionally locked, and youngsters are free to amble around on their own. Traffic is nonexistent, as vehicles are mostly left in parking lots outside institution grounds, and first-time visitors are excused if they think they have stepped into a wayback machine. Chautauqua feels like a world that existed half a century ago. The way many folks wish the world still felt like today.

All of that appeals to me as I enjoy my week in Chautauqua, just one of more than 170,000 people who will come throughout the summer. Then, there is the golf, 36 holes smartly routed among gentle, wooded hills, with vistas of Lake Chautauqua in the distance. The golf club opened in 1896, and early members built their own 9-hole course. Later, they commissioned Donald Ross to transform it into a more formidable 18-holer, and he did that, via topographical maps and photos and without ever visiting. The result is an easygoing track that is as accommodating to novice players as it is to those with single-digit handicaps. And as fun.

I relish the games I play each day on that layout, dubbed the Lake Course, and also the neighboring Hill Course, which came fully online in 1994. My playing partner regaled me with stories of how one year Willie Nelson wouldn't come off the Lake until right before he was scheduled to go on stage, and how much Vince Gill and Amy Grant enjoy the track each time they come to Chautauqua to perform. I also listened to tales of games played here years ago by Ben Hogan and Walter Hagen as well as Byron Nelson and Sam Snead. But the best story is the one of Amelia Earhart landing her plane on what is now the 17th fairway when she came up here to speak.

Cooperstown was the third stop on my Empire State jaunt, and it is always a pleasure to visit that bucolic burg of some two thousand people, which I have gotten to know quite well over the years. It's a place that has long been about baseball and books for me. Baseball because it is the site of the game's Hall of Fame, a must-visit for any fan of the national pastime, and also Doubleday Field, built on the cow pasture where Abner Doubleday is said to have invented the national pastime in 1839. And books because Cooperstown is the home of James Fenimore Cooper, author of such classics as *The Deerslayer* and *The Last of the Mohicans* and America's first literary star. Cooper's father, William, founded the village in 1786, and his writer son set many of his stories in the nearby woods and waters.

But after playing several rounds on the scenic Leatherstocking Golf Course, I have decided that Cooperstown is also a very special place to tee it up.

Devereux Emmet built the par-72 track in 1909 and named it after the character Natty Bumppo, who appeared in several of Cooper's books, and all these years later it retains the feel of an old-time course. Neatly integrated into the village, as a British Isles layout might be, Leatherstocking is not particularly long, measuring less than 6,500 yards from the back tees. The greens are small, the angles off the tees interesting, the bunkering deft, and the holes routed smartly up, down, and around the rolling hills and along sections of Lake Otsego. The par-three 3rd is a favorite of mine, with a green guarded by half a dozen bunkers and backed by the Fenimore Art Museum, a stylish neo-Georgian structure built where Cooper's old farmhouse used to stand. The 4th hole is notable not only for being a tough yet fair five-par with an especially challenging second shot that must clear a cluster of bunkers 120 yards from the green, but also for running along the Farmer's Museum. And I am equally distracted and delighted by the sight of people scurrying about the grounds of that attraction in nineteenth-century period dress as I try to play my shots. Partway through my round, my playing partner, who happens to be a native of Cooperstown, tells me how the land on which the first eight holes of the course are constructed reminds him of illustrations from Cooper's books.

Emmet knew how to work with good golf land, as he demonstrated in designing a pair of US Open courses in Garden City Golf Club on Long Island and Congressional Country Club in Washington, DC. And he showed that skill at Leatherstocking as well. I was especially enthralled with the finish. No. 15 is a burly five-par that begins with a drive toward the lake, Cooper's fabled "glitterglass," and 16 a shortish par-four that requires a precise iron to a green fronted by a creek. The 17th is a testy par with water running down the entire right side of the hole, and No. 18 is a bit of Pebble Beach in upstate New York, with a tee box set on a man-made island in the lake and a fairway that horseshoes around the lake to a green cut in the shadow of the stately Otesaga Inn and its inviting veranda.

It was my final round on a fabulous trip that demonstrated just how big golf is all over New York.

19

THE LOW COUNTRY
Chilling on the Golf Coast

IT WAS NOVELIST PAT CONROY WHO FIRST TURNED ME ON to the pleasures of the Low Country and the calming aura of those coastal lands. And as he wove his tales of his highly dysfunctional family, Conroy also conveyed a deep enchantment for the area where those books were based. For the rugged watermen who harvest shrimp, crab, and oysters from its bountiful waters. For the swathes of yellow-brown marshland and the creeks that cut through them. For the graceful lanes of its seaside towns, canopied by towering live oaks, their gnarly branches draped with Spanish moss. For the rows of stately antebellum houses with their picket fences. And for a style of life that seems a little slower and just a bit easier than anywhere else. It always sounded like a place where I wanted to linger, and when I finally found my way to the Low Country for the first time, I understood just why Conroy adored it—and why he wanted to reside there, even as it held so many troubled memories for him. The rhythms of the tides and winds, the sights of water birds and working boats plying the bays and sounds, and the salty smell of the sea air instantly tantalized me. And I relished the sense of life being so much simpler there.

I also loved that the area, which stretches from the northern reaches of South Carolina to southern Georgia, possessed some pretty good golf. And nowhere in that region is the golf better than at Sea Island, which is situated about an hour's drive north of Jacksonville, Florida.

The Sea Island resort features three golf courses, starting with Seaside and Plantation, a pair of superb, 18-hole designs that were revamped in the late 1990s—and that hosted the 2004 US Mid-Amateur Championship. Tom Fazio created Seaside from two disparate nines—one designed by the fabled team of Harry Colt and Charles Alison in the late 1920s and the other by Joe Lee in the early 1970s—while Rees Jones redesigned Plantation, which was originally laid out by Walter Travis in 1927. Both layouts are situated on a former cotton plantation and offer great variety in terms of shot making. Wind frequently blows hard off of Saint Simons Sound, often forcing players to go up or down two or three clubs, and it is also easy to get smitten by narrow footpaths of crushed oyster shells that snake through the tracks, the sculpted sand dunes that have formed in places, and the waving marsh grasses that are often in view. At certain times of the year, red and yellow wildflowers bloom on parts of the courses, and the creeks that twist through the land teem with redfish.

Just down the road from Seaside and Plantation is the golf course called Retreat. Originally constructed in the 1970s by Joe Lee, it was revamped in 2001 by longtime Sea Island resident Davis Love III. Brilliantly so. "We kept the old routing, but that was it," says Love. "We cut down trees and ripped up cart paths, the irrigation system, and all the grass. It had been a tight course before, and I wanted to give it some room off the tees and make it something even my mother and her friends could play, as well as elite players."

Of course, neither man nor woman can live by golf alone, and one of the beauties of Sea Island is all that it provides beyond the royal and ancient game. Start with the horseback rides down the seemingly endless stretch of beach, as ospreys soar above the waters and hermit crabs scurry across the bars. Massages are available in one of the twenty-six treatment rooms at the spa, and the shooting school offers skeet, trap, and sporting clays. There is fishing, too, and the runs of redfish and sea trout in the local waters can be strong.

The history of the Sea Island resort goes back to 1925, when Howard Coffin, the automotive mogul and founder of United Airlines, purchased what was essentially an uninhabited five-mile-long island. He and his cousin Alfred William Jones constructed a modest 9-hole golf course and hired noted Palm Beach architect Addison Mizner to design a sumptuous 270-room Mediterranean-style hotel that came to be called The Cloister. Over the next decades, the resort expanded to include parts of neighboring Saint Simons Island, where the Seaside, Plantation, and Retreat courses are located—and where Jones's grandson Bill oversaw the building in 2001 of The Lodge, a warm, 42-room abode where on-call butlers deliver milk and warm cookies to the rooms each evening. By the time that Jones finished an extensive renovation of The Cloister in 2006, Sea Island had evolved into a true luxury resort and was regarded as one of the finest golf destinations in the land.

Enthusiasm for the completed Cloister and a decade's worth of renovation work throughout the entire resort soared when the hotel reopened. But those emotions were soon replaced by despair when the economy began to tank in 2007 and Sea Island started choking on millions of dollars of debt. Things got so bad that the resort had to file for bankruptcy—and then had to sell to new owners.

Sadly, the Jones family lost control of the retreat they had so lovingly nurtured for three generations. But the folks who took over have treated it with comparable care, and Sea Island is in as good shape as it has ever been.

It is interesting to note, when one considers the recent travails of the resort, that Sea Island resort was founded before the start of the Great Depression—and endured its own difficulties through the tumult of the 1930s and then World War II. "Those were difficult times as well but the resort made it through them," says Jim Stahl, a longtime resident of Sea Island and the 1995 US Senior Amateur champion. "Well, times got tough again. But Sea Island has managed not only to survive but also move forward, continuing to do what it has long done so well. Which is entertaining guests and taking very good care of them."

Golfers who visit Hilton Head in South Carolina will find a place that strives to do much the same thing. To be sure, it is something of a different deal there, as that foot-shaped, 29,000-acre island is a much bigger destination and home to a number of different resorts as well as more than two dozen courses. It is also a busier retreat that caters to visitors of a broader demographic. But the place nonetheless projects the same sort of aura that makes the Low Country such a terrific place to kick back.

I think a lot about that when I play the great Harbour Town Golf Links, which was designed by Pete Dye. While I must confess to being a big fan of Pete's, I do not find his layouts particularly relaxing. Interesting, yes. Strategic and challenging, too. But the wild undulations of his greens often unnerve me, and so do his heaving fairways, which frequently send perfectly good shots into perfectly horrible positions. By his own admission, Dye likes to mess with golfers' heads, and it takes no amount of effort to get into mine when I try to discern the proper angles I should take off his tees.

But for some reason, I am completely at ease as I play my way around Harbour Town, a masterpiece that hosts an annual PGA Tour event. It's not the tiny greens on that perennial top one hundred track that have led me to that state, nor the fiendish bunkers and well-placed water hazards that make it so tough to shoot par. In fact, I am having a tough day as far as scoring goes. But I love being back in the Low Country, and at this spot, which is about twelve miles long and five miles wide and located equidistant between Savannah and Charleston. In fact, I am so lulled by my return to these parts that as I play the often-photographed 18th hole at Harbour Town and gaze at the brick red-and-white lighthouse that looms behind the green, I worry not one bit about what is a rather daunting approach.

I have come to Hilton Head with a foursome of friends, and Harbour Town is but one of several courses we sample during our stay. Earlier in the week, we teed it up at another difficult yet delightful Dye design, Heron Point, which has many of the same features and feels of that track, though it seemed a tad tighter. After that we played the heralded Robert Trent Jones course at Palmetto Dunes, which was constructed in 1967 and boasted lots of room off the tees and big, receptive greens. Then, we came to Harbour Town, which opened two years later. And while our days were filled with golf, we spent our evenings dining on sweet shrimp and savory barbeque at local eateries and then lingering after hours on the terrace at our very comfortable quarters at one of the so-called plantations, smoking cigars, savoring wine, and swapping stories well into the night.

We could have played tennis, if we were so inclined, as Hilton Head boasts some 350 courts. Or taken long walks on its beaches. Biking and hiking are major pastimes here, as is boating and fishing. And there are a number of historic points of interest, from old forts and plantation ruins to ancient shell rings. But as was the case on Sea Island, golf was the primary object of our affection at this stop.

The history of Hilton Head goes back several centuries, to 1663 to be specific, when an Englishman named William Hilton sailed into the region on a ship named *Adventure* and named a headland near the entrance to Point Royal Sound after himself. He was so enchanted by the area that he stayed there for several days. At that time, Native Americans occupied the isle on a seasonal basis, but then the British moved in, setting up indigo and cotton plantations. The Civil War brought that era to a close, as Hilton Head became an important Union army base and a place from which it enforced a blockade of the Southern ports, especially Savannah and Charleston. During that time, and after the conflict between the States had ceased, hundreds of ex-slaves moved to Hilton Head Island. They came to be known as the Gullah, or Geechee, and they led a mostly agrarian existence, farming, hunting, and fishing to support and sustain themselves. They also retained strong ties to their African heritages, and the isolation of the Low Country well into modern times enabled the Gullah to preserve much of their linguistic and cultural identity.

For many years through the late 1800s and well into the twentieth century, wealthy industrialists used huge sections of Hilton Head as a private hunting preserve. But then a group of timber investors purchased that property, and in the early 1950s they opened a trio of lumber mills. At the time, the island had a total population of three hundred people, and the only access was through private boats. A state-run ferry began operations in 1953, and three years later, a two-lane toll swing bridge came online, allowing automobile access for the first time. That span remained in operation until 1982, when the four-lane bridge that exists today replaced it.

Not surprisingly, the opening of the first bridge from the mainland to Hilton Head Island nearly sixty years ago spurred its development as a tourist destination. A fellow named Charles Fraser created the Sea Pines Resort, which would come to include Harbour Town and Heron Point, and others followed. Such as Palmetto Dunes, Shipyard, and Port Royal. These residential communities came to be known as "plantations" and were designed to accommodate homeowners as well as guests who could select from properties included in a rental pool. Those retreats also included various recreational amenities, including golf, and the first course on the island opened in 1961. Hilton Head grew quickly after that, and with the addition of several hotels. But thanks to Fraser, who considered himself a serious environmentalist, the island and its leaders strove to retain a strong semblance of its former isolated self even as it got bigger and busier. Streetlights were discouraged, to cut down on light pollution, and buildings were painted in very similar neutral tones. Corporate development was dissuaded, too, as was the installation of what would have been very visible offshore oil platforms.

Today, Hilton Head is a much different island than the one Fraser first began developing in 1956. Its total year-round population is thirty-eight thousand, and it hosts some 2.2 million visitors each year. Many of those folks stay in the more than sixty-four hundred rental homes and villas and thirteen hotels and inns. And it is in the middle of a renovation boom in which a number of the plantations and hotels are spending big bucks to upgrade facilities that had gotten somewhat tired.

While the place has surely grown over the years, I feel none of that development as I finish up my round at Harbour Town. Standing behind the 18th green, I gaze across

Calibogue Sound and savor the sights of the marsh grass being pulled and pushed by the wind.

At that moment, I realize I have once again succumbed to the calming rhythms of the Carolina Low Country. And not even Pete Dye can rattle me.

Before I head back north, I decide to visit the town of Beaufort, South Carolina, which is the place where Pat Conroy did so much of his writing. This charming coastal burg is also where parts of his best-selling novels, *The Prince of Tides* and *The Great Santini,* were set. In addition, some twenty movies have been shot here over the years, including cinematic adaptations of those two books as well as *The Big Chill* and *Forrest Gump.*

Chartered in 1711, Beaufort is the second oldest city in South Carolina, after Charleston, and it is hard not to feel that history when I wander the area known as the Point. This is the swell part of town, which has a total population of twelve thousand, and I head right to 1 Hancock Street. It's where the Meechum family of *The Great Santini* lived, and a few years later it served as the home of the Kevin Kline and Glenn Close characters in *The Big Chill.* Later on, I come upon the elegant white house with Ionic columns where the mother of the Nick Nolte character in *The Prince of Tides* resided, and all I want to do this afternoon is repose in a wicker chair on one of the two porches that run the entire front of the second and third floors and gaze across the Intracoastal Waterway that runs before it.

In describing Beaufort, Conroy talks about how everything happens in slow motion there, and enchantingly so. It is that way throughout the Low Country, from Sea Island to Hilton Head and everything in between. Which is why I keep coming back.

THE OUTPOSTS

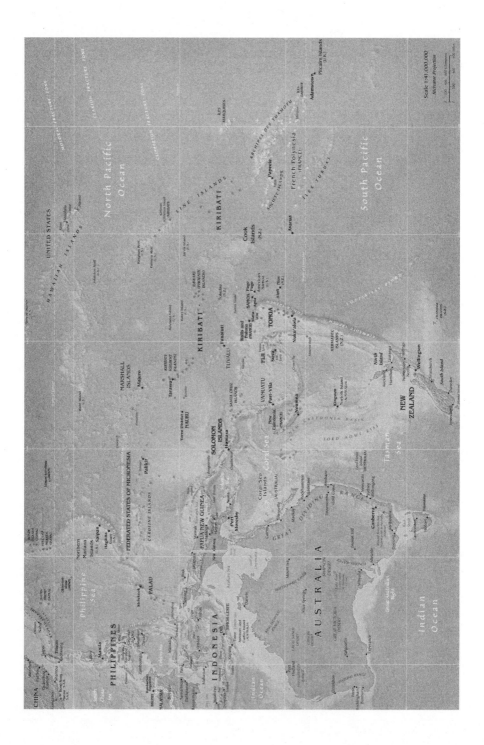

20

MOROCCO
Golf in the Kingdom

THE FAIRWAYS LOOK THE SAME AS THE ONES BACK HOME, and so do the bunkers and greens. But most everything else about my round at the Royal Marrakesh Golf Club is decidedly different. First, there is my drive to the course down a narrow asphalt highway that I have to share with goats, camels, mopeds, and donkeys pulling carts of fresh mint. I pass groves of date palms, gawking all the while at roadside merchants selling everything from fresh olive oil and live chickens to radios and kitchen pots. Once I start playing, on holes routed in the shadows of the snow-covered Atlas Mountains and by rows of apricot, orange, and olive trees, a lady in a black chador, the religious attire that many Muslim women wear in public, scampers mysteriously across the fairway in front of me and then disappears into the woods. I also watch an attendant at this course, which was built in 1933 by the Pasha of Marrakesh after he had become hooked on the

game, drop to his knees to pray by one tee after hearing the
muezzin call the faithful to a local mosque. My caddie speaks
only French and Arabic, and one of the men in the pro shop
tells me he had four wives.

Welcome to the North Africa monarchy of Morocco. A
predominantly Islamic land of some thirty million people,
it is a place chock full of the exotic, with mountain casbahs,
Roman ruins, and crowded souks. It also happens to be a hot-
bed of golf, with roughly thirty courses, several of which were
designed by top architects like Jack Nicklaus, Gary Player, and
Robert Trent Jones.

Golf bloomed in Morocco for one primary reason. Its
longtime leader, the late King Hassan II, was a golf fanatic.

Not only did he tee it up as often as royal duties allowed, but he also carried a single digit handicap for much of his adult life—thanks in no small part to his first engaging Claude Harmon, the former Winged Foot and Seminole Golf Club professional and 1948 Masters champion, and later Hall of Famer touring pro Billy Casper as his personal instructors. His Majesty also believed that golf could serve as a catalyst for developing tourism in his predominantly Islamic realm, believing that traveling golfers would spend more money than average tourists. So he instigated the construction of more than a dozen courses during his thirty-eight-year reign, including a handful within the walls of some of his palaces.

He built some very solid tracks, the best of which is the Red Course at the Royal Dar Es Salaam Golf Club outside the capital city of Rabat, which Trent Jones routed through a lush cork forest. The site for many years of an annual European PGA Tour event, the Hassan II Trophy, it boasts a challenging mix of long and short holes that compels players to work the ball as it also enchants them with a garden-like setting and a potpourri of on-course aromas from coppices of orange and mimosa trees as well as rose and hibiscus bushes. Then, there are the two-thousand-year-old columns from the ancient city of Volubilis that rise between the 11th and 12th holes, and the flocks of ibises, a bird sacred to Islamic theology, that frequently fly overhead. And forget about ever finding a bad lie there; the greenskeeping staff numbers four hundred people.

King Hassan II, who ascended to the throne in Morocco in 1961, died in 1999. But his nation's passion for golf remains strong under the patronage of his successor—and eldest son—King Mohammed VI as well as Crown Prince Moulay Rachid. Several acclaimed layouts have recently come online, and there are plans for several others. They are designed to sate recent rises in demand from golfers looking for different places to play the game. They are attracted by the high quality courses, to be sure. But they are also lured by Morocco's vibrant culture, which is an olio of Arab, Berber, Moorish, Jewish, and French influences, and enchanted by a friendly populace that likes to remind American visitors that in 1786 Morocco became only the second country, after France, to recognize the newly formed United States of America. Tourists are also taken by the scenic and varied terrain that includes towering mountains, vast deserts where movies such as *Lawrence of Arabia* have been filmed, and thirty-five hundred miles of beaches, as well as a very dry and temperate climate. And they fancy the kingdom's close proximity to Europe and the United States. London is only a three-hour flight away, while New York's JFK airport is reachable in roughly six hours. Shopkeepers converse easily in French, English, and Arabic, and the streets of Morocco's major cities, like Marrakesh, Rabat, Meknes, and Fez, are full of people wearing fezzes and flowing cotton robes called *djellabas*, as well as three-piece business suits. East and West, and North and South, seem to coexist quite easily here.

Perhaps the simplest way to break down golf in the kingdom is to divide the courses into four distinct categories that speak as much to the different ethos and geographies of those tracks as it does to their various locales. One encompasses those layouts in the Mediterranean region to the north, such as Tangier Royal Golf Club. Founded in 1914 when the leader of Morocco at the time, Moulay Abdelaziz, donated land on the outskirts of that city to members of the diplomatic community so they could build a course, it is the oldest in the country. Another category comprises what might be called the "cultural" segment and includes the courses in and around the Imperial Cities of Morocco— and the places where the sense of the country's traditions and history is strongest. Like Fez, the kingdom's spiritual and creative center, with 185 mosques, more than two hundred thousand resident artists, and a nifty 9-hole track. And Meknes, built in scrubby hills along vineyards and olive groves, and once known as the Versailles of Morocco. Moulay Ismail, the Alaouite sultan who ensured an even longer lasting legacy by fathering more than seven hundred sons, constructed many of its monuments and palaces in the late seventeenth century. The beguiling 9-hole golf course there came hundreds of years later.

A third designation belongs to those tracks in and around the Atlas Mountains, where the hoary crags of that majestic range come into view throughout most rounds. Marrakesh is the leading destination in this group, with several notable golf clubs within easy drives of this eleventh-century walled city. And the final cluster comprises the so-called sea courses near the Atlantic Ocean resort of Agadir, where morning rounds are followed by afternoons lazing on sun-drenched beaches.

Even after six trips to Morocco, I still have a hard time picking a favorite track. The Red Course at Royal Dar Es Salaam is undeniably the best of the bunch. But I also enjoy the course at Royal Meknes. It is not nearly as good from a design or conditioning standpoint, but what makes it well worth a visit is its location within the three-hundred-year-old walls of one of the late king's palaces. It is hard not to gawk at the ramparts that rise all around that layout, or at the Moorish gate by the 4th tee through which His Majesty used to walk onto the course from his residence. I also like the views of the minarets looming above the medina in the background as well as the colonnades and crenellated towers that rise so close to the action. I will never forget one round there when my playing partner sliced his drive on the first hole so badly that it went screaming over the wall to our right, and out of sight. "That's OP," I said. "Out of Palace. You had better reload." Players may unwind with a postround tour of the nearby ruins of the once prosperous Roman outpost of Volubilis, which thrived before the time of Christ. The well-preserved baths, columns, mosaics, and sculptures are something to behold, and so is the experience of wandering down the main street of this ancient settlement in your golf shoes, accompanied only by a random herd of sheep.

I also delight in playing in and around Marrakesh, for the golf, of course, but also for the many things I can do there after my games. I am particularly taken by the souk in that city, a dazzling maze in which merchants hawk everything from cactus honey and dried dates to caftans and leather bags as Arabic music pours out of rundown tape decks and wispy clouds of incense waft through the air. Entire stands are devoted to spices, with colorful sacks of paprika, thyme, and lavender laid out in neat rows.

Equally good is the so-called Square of the Dead, or Jemaa el Fna. Relatively quiet for most of the day, it comes alive at dusk, filling with local vendors and out-of-town visitors who turn it into a sort of North African country fair. Snake charmers lull deadly asps into trances in one area, and child boxers fight it out in another. Acrobats turn somersaults, and trained monkeys perform tricks. Fortune-tellers huddle under black umbrellas to share their visions of the future as musicians from Sub-Saharan Africa known as *gnawa* sing and dance to their rhythmic tunes. Rows of food stalls are suddenly assembled, and they pour smoke and steam into the early-evening air as they offer foods like sheep's heads and snails, lentil soup, and tripe. One place serves an array of "salads," in actuality a form of Moroccan tapas that includes smoky eggplant marinated in fresh olive oil and delicate carrots doused with rose water. Another stand peddles tagine of lamb with crushed grapes and almonds, followed by couscous with cooked vegetables.

I love Morocco for the golf. And for everything else I can do there.

21

FIJI
The Land of Yes

MATH HAS NEVER BEEN MY STRONG SUIT, WHICH IS WHY I assiduously avoided any classes involving numbers in school. But I quickly realize I do not have to be an MIT professor to figure out the staff-to-guest ratio at this ultraexclusive South Pacific resort that has just been revealed to me—and to appreciate how extraordinary it really is.

Laucala Island has a staff of 330, the resort's general manager says. And its maximum number of guests is 80. That's four staffers per guest, I quickly calculate. And then I listen to the general manager explain the simple benefits of that. "You never have to book a reservation for anything here," she says. "You never have to wear a watch. You only need to tell us what you want to do and when you want to do it. We will always be ready for you."

Now *that* is what I call welcoming. As welcoming as the azure waters of the Pacific and lush green hills of this private,

3,500-acre island that is protected by an eighteen-mile-long, horseshoe-shaped reef. As welcoming as the hilltop spa that makes its own lotions and oils. As welcoming as the David McLay Kidd course that charms golfers of all abilities with its downhill tee shots, its pleasing mix of long and short par-fours, its frequent glimpses of the ocean, and its sheer emptiness, for it rarely records more than a few rounds a day. And as welcoming as the five restaurants and seven lounges that seemingly exist for you and you alone—private retreats that treat the appearance of any guest as if he were there on a state visit—and then artfully prepare Michelin Star–worthy food and drink.

It's not just that a trip to Laucala Island seems like you are stepping into one of those beguiling paintings by Paul Gaugin—and makes you feel as if you have suddenly and sensibly fled civilization much as the post-Impressionist master did, to a gorgeous tropical setting where you can live, in his words, "on fish and fruit." Or that it offers every possible recreation to fill your hours here, be it scuba diving or snorkeling, golf or fishing, sailing or horseback riding—as well as the opportunity to simply while away your time by your pool or on your beach. It's that this new resort, which was developed by Red Bull energy drink cofounder Dietrich Mateschitz on an isle the reclusive Austrian bought from the family of Malcolm Forbes nearly a decade ago, offers a level of service that is unattainable most anywhere else.

It is the "Land of Yes," a friend of mine states. I offer that the word "no" does not exist here. And we both agree that attitude makes Laucala a true tropical paradise.

To be sure, this paradise costs a bundle, with the twenty-five villas on the property going for anywhere from $3,800 to $30,000 an evening. You can even rent out the whole island for $150,000 a night (and someone has already done that for four nights next year). That sounds like a lot, and it is. But one of the most accurate adages in life is this: you get what you pay for. And you get a lot at Laucala.

Among other things, you get a warm greeting at the island airfield when you fly in from Fiji's main airport at Nadi, with a couple dozen staffers singing for you as you step onto the tarmac. You get a quiet and remote island where guests and staffers are the only occupants. You get villas designed in traditional Fijian style, with thatch roofs, stone walls, and wood beams held together with traditional coconut matting called *magi-magi*. Each abode comes with its own pool, as well as indoor and outdoor showers and baths and outside daybeds and chaise lounges. A wireless Internet connection keeps you from feeling that far away from home, even if you are halfway around the world, and so does the impeccable cell service. Some villas hang like tree houses over the beach, and they all look over the water. Remnants of the old coconut palm plantations still exist on the island, and stands of papaya, banana, and cinnamon trees flourish. Most of the food you eat is harvested from the resort's own farm, including the beef, chicken, goats, and lamb (which comes from a breed of sheep called Fiji Fantastic for the way it naturally—and remarkably—sheds its wool).

Fiji itself is pretty fantastic, an English-speaking nation of nine hundred thousand people located just over the International Dateline and consisting of more than three hundred islands, of which a third are uninhabited. Its mild tropical climate makes it a place worth visiting any time of year, though the optimum time may be during the dry season, also known as the Fijian Winter, which runs from May to October. And its soothing tropical ethos makes it a place where the stresses of everyday life wash away easily with the sun and sea.

Those attributes are no doubt part of what drew Mateschitz to Laucala Island. And he has made that attraction even greater by augmenting it with five-star service. Service you will have no difficulty realizing is better than most any place on earth. No matter how good or bad you are at math.

To give you an idea of what life on Laucala is all about, let me describe a typical day and night there. It begins when I am gently roused from my slumber by the rhythmic thuds of the wooden *lali* drum outside my thatched-roof *bure*. Traditionally, a *lali* was used to warn villagers of danger, like an impending attack from a neighboring island, or to gather them for a meeting or celebration, but on this morning, in this time, the drum serves simply as my alarm clock, and a member of the resort's staff is beating mine.

I am just getting out of bed when that staffer pours me a steaming cup of French press coffee. Then she asks: "Where do you want to take breakfast today?" I suggest the table on my expansive terrace, the one by the pool. She smiles as she nods and then begins to lay out my feast. I walk to my beach, just ten yards away, and dive into the salty, cerulean waters of the South Pacific Ocean. I look up to see islands rising in the distance, looming like snaggled shadows, and a slight breeze blows. Small waves break softly on the beach, the foamy white water running up the sand.

Breakfast is ready by the time I return, and I dig into a bowl of pineapple, watermelon, papaya, coconut, and oranges, all grown on the resort's farm. The pineapple is so sweet it tastes like dessert, and so juicy I have to keep dabbing at the sides of my mouth with my white linen napkin. I smear local Laucala honey across a freshly baked croissant, and by the time I finish my second cup of coffee, the morning sun has cleared the band of clouds on the horizon it had earlier turned the same brilliant red color of the chili bush flowers that grow around my *bure*.

Right after breakfast, I play a round on the 18-hole, David McLay Kidd golf course that winds in and around the hilly jungle and also along the island's sandy shores. The layout has a delightfully tropical feel, and I gawk at the groves of coconut palms that climb up the lush hills on either side of the fairways as well as the turquoise waters that come into view throughout the round. I particularly like the way Kidd has criss-crossed the 8th and 9th holes so that your drive on the par-three 9th is hit over the fairway of the par-five 8th. And I love the bunker he created around the 12th green that runs right onto the adjoining beach.

Heading back to my beach is all I can think about when I am done playing, as the temperature has climbed into the mid-80s. So I rush to my *bure* for another swim. Then I rinse off the seawater in one of my two outdoor showers before casting off for some deep-sea fishing.

Our boat is a stylish, forty-one-foot Riviera, and we only have to travel for forty minutes to get to what our guide James calls his favorite spot. There are four of us onboard, including James, Matthew the captain, and a cheerful fellow named Api who has a role that can best be described as "fishing butler." He not only proffers a lunch of sushi and spring rolls but also pours me a glass of sparking rose, which I savor as I sit in the fishing chair in the back of the boat. Suddenly, the line for one of the rods starts to whirr wildly, and as James rushes over to adjust the drag, Api deftly grabs the wine glass out of my hand so I can land what turns out to be a fifty-pound wahoo. And he spills nary a drop.

We land a few tuna that afternoon as well, and a mahi-mahi, and the best part of bringing those in was watching their luminous bodies darting frantically through the water as we pull them closer to the boat, the wahoo several shades of blue and the mahi-mahi a brilliant green-yellow. James alerts one of the resort chefs to our success, and he meets us at the dock. As the chef heads back to the kitchen to begin preparing the fish for the evening's dinner, I head up to the spa, nestled in the verdant hills near the golf course. I want a massage, though I do not have an appointment. Not to worry, the receptionist says, and she quickly arranges a relaxation treatment. I lapse in and out of consciousness as my masseuse works out all the kinks of a vigorous day's worth of golf and fishing, with oils made from coconuts that had been pressed a few hours before. Then I return to my room, for yet another outdoor shower, the water gushing from a head the size of a small manhole cover as frogs hop around my feet.

The first rum of the day is poured at 6 p.m., and mixed with pineapple juice squeezed before my very eyes. Then it is dinner. Tuna sashimi from the yellowtail I had caught, with fresh wasabi. Spicy tuna roll from the same fish. Grilled mahi-mahi. Grilled wahoo, too. All accompanied by a crisp New Zealand chardonnay and enjoyed at a beachside eatery with tables arrayed under the stars, the ocean only a chip shot away.

It is one of the best days of my life. And I cannot wait to do it all over again.

22

HAWAII
Living Large on the Big Island

I HAVE PLAYED SEVEN COURSES IN FIVE DAYS, AND enjoyed every round. But golf is the last thing on my mind as I settle into a potent rum drink at the Beach Tree Bar & Grill at the Four Seasons Hualalai Resort, listening to palm fronds rattle gently in the trade winds as the Pacific swallows the sun.

I think instead of the lava beds I have seen throughout the trip, the almost inconceivable stretches of jagged, charcoal-colored stones and boulders that line fairways and roads alike, and make this part of the Big Island feel like a moonscape. I also consider the lush rain forests in the nearby Pololu Valley, so overflowing with plant life that it would take a botanist an eternity to identify the different flora, and the funky artiness of the nearby town of Hawi, with its yoga studios and galleries playing Grateful Dead bootlegs. Then I savor a trip I took through the mountainous ranching region outside Waimea, where Hereford cattle wander in pastures sectioned off by barbed wire fences—and where local cow-boys known as *paniolos* tend to their stock.

I take another swig of my beverage, sweetly flavored with the juice from freshly picked pineapples, and recall the Hula Daddy coffee plantation I had wandered around the after-noon before, admiring the neat rows of bean-bearing trees that grow on lush green terraces fifteen hundred feet above the Pacific. During that outing, I had learned that coffee is, in many ways, king on the Big Island, and Hawaii has some eight hundred producers operating on land as small as a quarter acre and as large as five hundred acres. I also discovered that there is a wonderful coffee trail south of the Kona Airport for those caffeine addicts interested in sampling the many differ-ent brews. An afternoon there feels a lot like a trip through the wine country in, say, Sonoma or Napa, California, with tours and tastings for visitors. Only in this case, there are no issues with driving afterward.

I then focus for a bit on the four volcanoes that rise on this isle, some more than thirteen thousand feet high. They are occasionally dusted with snow, and the two that are still active frequently spew smoke that creates what locals call "vog," for volcanic fog. I smile when I consider walking part of the King's Trail, built through the lava beds here in the 1800s. Legend has it that King Kamehameha once declared that all travelers on this trail would be safe and protected, and he meted out harsh penalties to those who violated that decree. And while the trail long ago stopped serving as an important route for Big Island travelers, it stands today as an impressive historical site with petroglyphs dating back hun-dreds of years.

In time, I begin to contemplate the eateries I've checked out on this trip, from the small burger joint in Waimea serv-ing beef raised on area ranches to the elegant Pahu i'a res-taurant at the Four Seasons. Local ingredients are imperative, and so is making sure that the distance from farm and sea to table is as short as possible.

I almost drop my glass when I remember learning that the Big Island has eleven of the world's thirteen main climate zones, with environments ranging from desert plains and rain forests to snow-capped mountains and black-sand beaches. It's as if I have entered a real-life biosphere, and explains why it can be so arid around the golf courses on the coast and so wet up in the hills just a short drive away. And then I remind myself of another remarkable bit of information: that Hawaii is still growing, literally, thanks to the lava that continues to pour out of the Kilauea Caldera to the southeast.

Suddenly, I can't help wondering whether it is the rum that is making me forget exactly why I have come here, or the fact that this island simply has so much to offer.

Don't get me wrong. The golf on the Kohala Coast is quite good. One of the most celebrated tracks there is the Jack Nicklaus course at the Four Seasons that plays host to the Champions Tour season-opening tournament each year. Fairways snake lava fields there, and the Pacific is often in view. Especially on the par-three 17th, which backs up to the ocean, and the 18th, a dramatic finisher reminiscent of the final hole at Pebble Beach. Only on this hole, golfers have to carry an ancient Hawaiian fishpond to reach a fairway protected by bunkers all the way up the left side.

Just as good is the members-only course at Hualalai, called Ke'olu. The Tom Weiskopf layout is set farther back from the Pacific than the Nicklaus track and has more elevation changes. That gives me additional opportunities to gaze across the ocean waters, and I also marvel at the natural culverts I find at different spots, through which lava has flowed over the years on its way to the sea.

The Robert Trent Jones Sr. track at Mauna Kea, which features a Cypress Point–like par-three early in the round and plenty of scenic yet tough holes after that, is a winner, as is the rugged Hapuna course that Arnold Palmer and Ed Seay built in the scruffy hills above that layout. I also find the North and South Courses at nearby Mauna Lani big fun, especially when it comes to playing their seaside holes and savoring the visual contrasts of their emerald fairways against the blue-green Pacific and the sugar-white sand of their bunkers. The two tracks at Waikoloa, known as the King's and Beach courses, give me all I can handle when the wind blows, as it so often does, and I fall hard for the various looks and feels of their golf holes—and the sense that I never play the same one twice.

In many ways, the forty-mile-long Kohala Coast offers players a rich and varied menu of golf, with eight top-flight courses located within a twenty-minute drive of each other. Though it fairly pours in other parts of Hawaii, it rains only ten inches a year here, making the golfing weather as pleasant as it is predictable. And the course designs combine with the multiple teeing areas to give players great architectural variety. In addition, the resorts at which they operate cater to a wide range of travelers—whether well-heeled couples seeking the ultimate in privacy and luxury (Four Seasons), families as interested in value as quality (Waikoloa), and everything in between. Which means there is something for every ilk of traveler.

But it is the uniqueness of the locale and all a visitor can do on and off the course that really gets to me. There is also the matter of the Big Island as a whole, boasting an understated ambience that isn't all leis and luaus. To be sure, it has its fair share of tourists—and tourist traps, but it has also managed to retain a very true sense of its old-time self.

It is my first trip to Hawaii, and I suddenly wonder what took me so long to finally get here. Part of that surely has to do with its distance from my New England home. But it is also the result of my not being sure exactly which island to visit. I had heard good things about Oahu and Maui when it came to golf. Kauai, too. But people kept telling me about the Big Island.

I consider all this as I order another drink. Then I make the sort of lucid determination that seems to come so easily at cocktail hour.

I have got to find a way to get back.

23

AUSTRALIA AND NEW ZEALAND
Digging It Down Under

I HAVE LEARNED OVER YEARS OF FAIRLY EXTENSIVE travel that there are places so remarkable that a wanderer's impulse as he nears the end of his stay is not to leave but to send instead for his family. Destinations so interesting and warm, and so full of charm and beauty, that he is ready to move heaven and earth just to move there. Locales where the sense of discovery and adventure is high, the living is easy— and yes, the golf quite good.

As I walk off the 14th green at the Barnbougle Lost Farm course on the north coast of the Australian state of Tasmania, I realize I have found one of those special spots. It's the delight of playing the Bill Coore track there that grabs me first. A true links, Lost Farm boasts wide, undulating fairways; towering sand hills; testy green complexes guarded by gaping, blowout bunkers and heaving mounds; and a routing with such variety of distances and angles that I hit every club in my bag—and play about every kind of shot. It is also the pleasure of breathing salty sea air, regarding the water views of such natural splendor—and enjoying the occasional sight of tawny, pot-bellied wallabies standing by greens and along fairways, quizzically considering my presence.

The golf is great at Lost Farm, and also at its sister links, Barnbougle Dunes, laid out next door by another notable American designer, Tom Doak, and Australian architect Michael Clayton. In fact, the destination comprising those two tracks, which local cattle rancher and potato farmer Richard Sattler founded (with assists in financing and mentoring from Mike Keiser of Bandon Dunes fame), is a must-visit for golf connoisseurs. But it is not the only reason I want to resettle in this exotic state, which takes its name from the Dutch explorer Abel Tasman, who first came onto this land in 1642.

There is also the artsy ethos of Hobart, a former whaling station and now the scenic, waterfront capital of Tasmania and home to the delightfully wild and weird Museum of Old and New Art (MONA). I am enthralled by the beaches of Wineglass Bay near Coles Bay on the east coast, their fine sands endlessly massaged by waves from the Tasman Sea and backed by the imposing peaks of the Hazards Mountains. And enticed by outings such as the tour I take one afternoon of a working oyster farm on the Swan River in the northeast portion of the state. After donning a pair of chest waders, I follow my guide who leads me to a table set up in four feet of water. She then pops the cork in a bottle of sparkling Tasmanian wine she has been carrying in her daypack, and after pouring me a glass, starts shucking oysters she has just pulled out of the river. I eat half a dozen right out of their shells, deliciously briny and Reubenesque, as gulls soar overhead and fish jump.

The pastureland full of sheep and cattle in some parts of the land dazzle me, as do the rolling stands of timber replete with pines and country lanes shaded by arching gum and tea trees. Wine is prolific here as well, and I learn that Tasmania boasts some 240 vineyards. Whether red, white, or rose, they invariably impress with their tastes and characters, and I never lack for a proper glass.

A playing partner one day tells me that nearly forty percent of Tasmania, which is about the size of West Virginia, is covered by preserves and parks, and claims that the state affectionately called Tassie (pronounced "Tazzie") is known for having the cleanest air on the planet. His enchanting company reinforces one more revelation: the people of Tasmania, who are playfully mocked by mainlanders for being inbred yokels, are quite learned and up-to-date. Urbane and outdoorsy, too. They appreciate the good life, but they feel absolutely no need to pick up their pace of living to do so.

I e-mail my wife, Cynthia, back home in the States and suggest it is time for her and our daughters to pack.

She responds a few hours later, via Skype and with the knowing chuckle of a savvy spouse. "You've done this before," she said, reminding me of similar missives sent while I traveled to other Australian states in years past, and also to New Zealand. "So, which place will it be?"

Now, it is my turn to laugh, because I was not at all sure of what I should say. I love Aussie, to be sure. And New Zealand, too. "Maybe we can live in both places," I allow, understanding that my pronouncement is as unrealistic as it is understandable. Because being Down Under is simply that good.

I feel that way after only four days in Tassie, and those senses only became stronger after I head to South Australia, another of the island continent's states. I again fall hard for a pair of superb courses, only these are routed through the sand hills of the colonial city of Adelaide, set between the Mount Lofty ranges and Gulf St. Vincent and populated by just over a million people. One is the Royal Adelaide Golf Club, an acclaimed track that Dr. Alister MacKenzie modified during his famous 1926 visit to Australia, altering several holes so they better interacted with the dunes in the middle of the property. And the other is Kooyonga Golf Club, which was laid out on rolling land in 1922 by H. L. "Cargie" Rymill, a MacKenzie disciple and longtime Royal Adelaide member. The course boasts an intriguing mix of holes with tree-lined fairways and small, firm greens, and it gets props not only as an excellent members track but also as a place that has hosted five Australian Opens, including the one in 1965 that Gary Player won after shooting a pair of 62s.

My affection for South Australia only grows after a couple of days touring nearby vineyards of the McLaren Vale and the Barossa Valley, where English, German, and Italian settlers started making superlative wines in the 1830s. The McLaren has more than 100 growers, while the Barossa is populated with some 150 wineries, and they produce a number of stylish wines of superb quality and consistency. Grapes as wide ranging as Riesling and Merlot, Chardonnay and Grenache flourish there as does the star of Australia wine, Shiraz. Those grapes were among the first planted in the region, and they are among the oldest of that variety in the world. That's what gives them such a high intensity of alcohol and very full-bodied flavors. It is also one reason why the Penfolds Grange, a fantastic Bordeaux-style blend (only with Shiraz not Cabernet as the base) is one of the most celebrated wines on the planet.

To the east are the Australian states of Victoria and New South Wales, and they are home to a pair of scenic and eminently livable cities, Melbourne and Sydney, that bustle with intoxicating energy and cater to every possible cultural need and interest. They also possess some fabulous golf, including several courses either created or augmented by MacKenzie, whose US design credits include Cypress Point and Augusta National—and who frequently and quite deftly employed the concepts of military camouflage, learned as a civil surgeon in South Africa during the Boer War, in his work as a golf course architect. In fact, his 1926 visit to Australia, which was then considered a golfing backwater, was considered so significant that contemporary course designer Tom Doak has described it as one that "changed a continent." Doak, Jack Nicklaus, and Greg Norman are among those architects who have ensured that those states also have some first-rate modern courses, and the variety and depth of the layouts in those places are impressive.

I would hasten to add that New Zealand is just as compelling a golf destination. For stunning seaside courses like Kauri Cliffs and Cape Kidnappers. For the superb wines produced throughout that land, especially the Sauvignon Blancs of Hawke's Bay. For the breathtakingly varied and beautiful countryside that includes snow-covered mountains, dense forests, raging rivers, vast pasturelands, and beguiling bays. And for the quiet pace and hospitality of a spot populated by only 3.5 million very easygoing people.

The question is, how can Cynthia and I possibly choose between them all?

It's hard not to consider Tasmania quite seriously. The two courses at Barnbougle are nearly reason enough to relocate, a Down Under version of Bandon Dunes, with their simple airs and extraordinary designs. The one dubbed Barnbougle Dunes opened in 2004, and it winds among grassy dunes that rise and pitch along the Bass Strait. The course begins gently, with a modest five-par and then a trio of shortish yet stylish par-fours. Stepping off the 4th green, I gaze across the body of water that separates Tasmania from the mainland before walking along the dunes to the 5th tee, the sounds of waves crashing against the beach drowning out all else. "Now, this is fun!" I holler after I hit my tee shot on that 190-yard hole, and it is an expression I repeat throughout the round. It's the brilliant sequencing of the holes I like so much and the shots they force me to hit. Ditto the green complexes that reward you when you hit your approaches to the correct quadrants, and don't punish you too badly when you miss. Then, there are the visuals: the lush green of the fairways and greens contrasting to the pale brown marram grass and the oyster-white sand of the bunkers that pock the property; the expansive, almost cobalt-blue sky; and the cotton-white cumulus clouds filling parts of it.

The second course of Sattler's creation is called Lost Farm, and it came online two years ago. Created by Bill Coore, who worked solo on this project and not with his usual design partner Ben Crenshaw, who was otherwise engaged, the course takes its name from the pockets of pasture that used to form amid the shifting sand dunes and the ways that livestock used to become "lost" in those spots throughout that untamed land. I marvel at the short par-three 4th at Lost Farm, its green set on top of a dune above the beach. And I love the drive on the par-four 5th, a blind tee shot that is reminiscent of the drive on the Road Hole on the Old Course. Only you hit over a hefty sand dune here some sixty-feet high, and not over a section of a hotel. The bird and animal life is as exotic on this track as it is on the Dunes, with blue-tongued lizards the size of small dachshunds scurrying across tees and pink-tinted galahs, which are a sort of Australian cockatoo, squawking as they fly overhead. Just as unusual is the fact that Lost Farm has 20 holes, the extras being a pair of par-threes that are not only fun to play during a round but also fit perfectly with a track that deserves to be ranked among the top one hundred in the world. As does its neighbor.

The courses in Adelaide are not nearly as isolated as those in Tassie, nor quite as wild, for they are located within the city limits. But they are just as inviting. Linksy in nature and frequently buffeted by winds from not-too-distant seas,

Royal Adelaide is full of character, with small piney forests set along fairways and behind greens, as well as history. I like how a commuter rail still runs through the ground, and that the pro shop long ago served as a sort of rail station for Royal Adelaide members. I also cherish the story of a member who was one day so frustrated with his game that he pushed his clubs and his pull cart into the path of the train. Seconds later, the story goes, it was raining irons and woods.

Kooyonga merits as much praise for its design and conditioning as Royal Adelaide. It starts with a pair of throat-clearing par-fives, and then takes the golfer on a trip up and around the sand hills that rise in the middle of the property. The shot value is superb, and so is its location, a mere ten minutes by car to the Adelaide Airport. That makes it the perfect course to end a stay here.

If I were to pick anywhere to go from the South Australia capital, it would probably be Melbourne and its glorious sand belt about forty-five minutes out of town. That is where one finds the so-called Seven Sisters, a collection of classic golf clubs with rich histories, fine courses, and in the majority of cases, architectural input from MacKenzie himself.

The most famous of those tracks is the West at Royal Melbourne, and it is rightfully regarded as the best in Australia. Built on well-contoured land with sandy soil that drains well, the course features wide fairways, bold bunkering, and massive greens. Conditioning is generally superb, and it is hard not to recognize design similarities in some of the holes there. Standing over a shot on the 10th hole on the West one day, I cannot help but feel I have been suddenly transported to Augusta National. And the green complexes of a couple of holes are very reminiscent of Cypress Point.

MacKenzie did not lay out the East Course at Royal Melbourne. But the gentlemen who did—club member Alex Russell and course superintendent Mick Morum—had worked closely with the Good Doctor on his design of the West and actually constructed that track after the architect left the country. As a result, they were able to produce something quite similar and special, and the courses meld together so well from a design standpoint that a composite layout of the two tracks is used whenever significant championships are staged at Royal Melbourne, such as the President's Cup in 1998 and 2011, and fifteen Australian Opens over the years.

MacKenzie also performed quite a bit of work on the bunkering at Kingston Heath, which is located just down the road. And he had architectural input on three other members of the Seven Sisters: the Victoria, Metropolitan, and Yarra Yarra Golf Clubs. They are essential stops, as are the final two courses in that group, Commonwealth and Huntingdale.

Sydney is also worth a visit, for its gorgeous opera house and magnificent harbor as well as its chic shopping and stylish dining scene. There is also the course that MacKenzie designed at its New South Wales Golf Club. Laid out on a windswept finger of land that overlooks Botany Bay, where Captain James Cook sailed into Australia aboard the *Endeavor* in 1770, it evokes all the drama and natural beauty of Cypress Point. The architect made terrific use of the sharp ridges that run through the property as well as the rugged coastline, and it is little wonder that his creation at New South Wales is regularly ranked among the top fifty courses in the world.

While golf has always been the impetus for my travels to Australia, the trips have always been about much more than the royal and ancient game. It is an easygoing place in many ways, with the sort of can-do, pioneering spirit that America possessed a century ago. Aussies enjoy their sports and their beers, and they are certainly an active bunch. Animal life abounds when one leaves the exceedingly pleasant cities of that nation, and I often came upon kangaroos and wallabies wandering across fairways and greens, and saw a few sleepy koalas clinging to eucalyptus trees. I chuckled at the strange names of creatures I occasionally encountered in the wild, such as birds called galahs and kookaburras, and marveled at the equally exotic appellations I found on the menus, like marrons and yabbies, which are species of shellfish. I also fretted about the many insects and reptiles that can kill you in Australia. In fact, most of the literature I digested about the country before traveling there for the first time contained so many warnings about poisonous snakes and spiders that they read like those terrifying medical disclaimers that so often come with purchases of prescription drugs. I had started to believe that I would be lucky to survive the trip. I thought it strange that such a friendly place would have such deadly denizens. Needless to say, I was careful not to venture too deep into the rough for golf balls that had flown a bit off course.

Such worries aside, I have managed to make it through four visits to Australia with nary a trip to the emergency room. And I always made an effort to see as much as I could off golf course. One day, for example, I walked on the beach at the Seal Bay Conservation Park on Kangaroo Island's south shore, just a puddle jump away from Adelaide Airport. The preserve is home to a colony of perhaps five hundred Australian sea lions, and at any given time about half of that bunch are out in the sea, spending as many as seventy-two sleepless hours feeding before dragging themselves back to the beach to sleep and recover. My guide led me up and down the beach for an hour or so, and we stepped carefully between the seals strewn across the sand like abandoned automobiles, resting up for their next feeding trip into the sea.

The courses in New Zealand are not as varied or plentiful as those in Australia, and they do not possess the sort of historical significance that comes from the involvement of a golf heavyweight like Alister MacKenzie. But North Island layouts such as Kauri Cliffs and Cape Kidnappers, which are located at the two five-star resorts of those same names built by American financier Julian Robertson, make it a golfer's paradise, as do tracks like Kinloch by Lake Taupo and Paraparaumu, just outside Wellington. As for the South Island, The Hills and Jack's Point provide all the golfing pleasure a player could possibly desire. Nearby, guests of the Matakauri Lodge, owned and operated by Robertson, have full access to the courses at The Hills and Jack's Point. Located on the shores of Lake Watatipu and backdropped by the hoary peaks of the Remarkables mountain range, it is a luxurious yet cozy and quiet retreat that features only eleven suites.

But in many ways, the golf is secondary here, for New Zealand often feels like one big national park that is crying out for its visitors to trek and ski, fish and paraglide, bicycle and bungee jump and just savor its extraordinary settings in every possible way.

One outing I will never forget is the kiwi walk I took with a naturalist while staying at Cape Kidnappers. Kiwis are the national birds of New Zealand, and they are odd-looking beings, brownish and big-billed with feather-like hair. They are also charmingly benign and extremely vulnerable to the sorts of predators that settlers have introduced to the country over the years, particularly feral cats. So people like Julian Robertson, the owner of the Cape Kidnappers resort, have gone to great lengths to save the birds. One such effort is the rather pricey and eminently enjoyable kiwi walk, during which my guide and I tracked a pair of those birds, each of which possessed electronic transmitters. The glee of actually finding the kiwis, and then holding them for a brief period, was as satisfying as acing a short par-three.

I still don't know where Cynthia and I are going to live.

24

NICARAGUA AND COSTA RICA

Latin Lovers

THE WAY I SEE IT, GOLF IS MORE THAN JUST A SPORT when I take my game on the road. It is also an adventure, and I'm not only talking about the escapades that come from errant swings and the off-the-grid places I often hit my shots. I also mean the experience itself.

I consider that conclusion as I walk toward the 14th green on the pleasurable, Mike Young golf course at the Hacienda Pinilla resort in Guanacaste, Costa Rica. As the waters of the cobalt-blue Pacific are roiling behind the hole as a result of the twenty-knot wind, I think about my round up to this point. And I realize that this Central America republic offers plenty in the way of adventure for golfers.

First, there is the sound of my playing partner hollering this morning as he scours the rough for a badly pulled drive: "Hey, I almost stepped on an iguana!" I look over to see him perform the sort of frantic backpedal one might expect from an NFL cornerback trying to cover an All-Pro receiver on a slant. But with much less athleticism. A couple of holes later, a pair of howler monkeys screech at me from a mango tree by a green. And when I howl back, one of them tosses a mango at my feet.

The sense of the exotic is only enhanced by the tropical dry forest that lines most of the holes here, and the cacophony of bird calls that wafts out of vegetation so thick it obscures the source of the sounds, but thankfully not the sounds themselves. Occasionally, I hear what I assume are animals crashing through the thickets, but I cannot see them and have no idea what they might be. Which is probably for the better, as I wonder whether I can stave off a charging boar with a Titleist 913 driver.

By the time we play No. 15, a dramatic par-three that requires a short iron to a green set right on the edge of a beach and backed by waters that loom like a giant, drive-in movie screen, I remember the surfers I had watched that morning, catching waves off the nearly empty beaches to the south that stretch nearly four miles long. I also recall the riders galloping horses in the sand at sunrise and the snorkelers plying the nearby reefs for up close and personal glimpses of Technicolor marine life.

I feel the same way about Costa Rica's neighbor to the north and west, Nicaragua, where I had just spent an equally enjoyable week, playing golf, savoring superb cigars and otherworldly rum, and relishing the occasional swim and Swedish massage at the newly opened Mukul resort on that nation's sun-drenched Emerald Coast—and also getting a sense of life in less well-heeled parts of that one-time revolutionary state, which is still run by one of the leaders of the Sandinistas that took over the land in the early 1980s, Daniel Ortega.

What's not to love about Latin American golf?

Costa Rica has built a reputation over the years as a place to go for adventure, and it is pretty well developed in that regard. The sport fishing and zip-lining has been good and quite popular for some time. The same can be said for birding, surfing, and overall ecotouring. Now, golf is making a play as yet one more reason to head to this former Spanish colony, which gained its independence in 1838—and constitutionally abolished its military in 1949. And as I was discovering, playing golf here truly is an adventure, which seems only right in a place that is all about adventure.

Perhaps the strongest course in the land is Hacienda Pinilla, where the layout was built on gentle rolling land that once served as a cattle ranch and is now part of a 4,500-acre resort. Young very sensibly designed the track to play like a links, given how often the wind blows, and he made it conform to the slopes and contours of the natural landscape. It opened in the winter of 2001 and has matured into a course that is as fun as it is challenging.

Another formidable Costa Rica track is the Robert Trent Jones Jr. layout at Reserva Conchal. Constructed in 2004 on rolling hills that offer sweeping ocean views, it is part of a 2,500-acre Westin resort that boasts two miles of coastline. The howler monkeys were also out in force when I visited Conchal, which has a nice mix of holes and demands that players hit a variety of shots. Only these primates did not throw anything at me and seemed to content themselves instead by screeching. The big surprise was the mysterious emergence at dusk of dozens of *pizotes*, small mammals closely related to raccoons but resembling anteaters. These strange-looking creatures began foraging for food in rather large numbers along the fairways, by the greens, and around the clubhouse as I was finishing play; they seemed utterly unafraid of human presence. A couple of them walked so close to me at times that they brushed up against my pants, and it didn't faze them a bit. I, however, nearly jumped out of my shoes.

Then I teed it up at the Four Seasons Peninsula Papagayo, where the Arnold Palmer golf course is routed on top of a massive plateau that overlooks the glistening waters of Bahia de Culebra. It feels like a Latin American version of Old Head in Ireland, and the bird and plant life of Papagayo is so interesting and exotic that I felt I needed experts in ornithology and botany to accompany me on my round. I especially enjoyed watching the parrots, as brightly colored as highlighters, frolic in the trees, along with the toucans, with their brilliantly hued beaks. The golf was very strong, too, and I was particularly taken with the 6th, a longish four-par that plays from an elevated tee to a fairway some two hundred feet below, and then to a green set on the edge of a cliff.

My enjoyment of those rounds came as much from the adventure of it all as it did the golf. I found that part of the adventure in visiting Costa Rica entails understanding the lifestyle.

They have a great expression here: *Pura vida.* Literally, it means the "pure life," but it can be used and translated in a variety of ways. As a greeting, for example, and that's how many people responded to me during my stay at La Posada, the boutique hotel made up of small casitas at Hacienda Pinilla, or wherever I lounged in the infinity pool at the Beach Club there or teed it up on any of the aforementioned courses. As if they want to be sure I enjoy the pure life while I am here. Or more accurately, the good life. Folks also use *pura vida* as a sort of adjective. If you were to say: "I'm going surfing today," they might respond: "*Pura vida.*" Like a stoner dude saying: "Excellent." The phrase is a way of saying everything is cool, and it also is how people here describe the relaxed ethos.

Speaking of excellent, nothing I did off the golf course was quite as good as those times I ventured to a wide expanse of sand called Playa Avellanas. After taking a dip in the Pacific, cool enough to be comfortable yet plenty refreshing, I would stroll along the water to an idyllic beachside retreat called Lola's. There, wooden tables, high-back chairs, and hammocks are arrayed under rustling palms; the sounds of five-foot waves breaking in the distance almost drowned out by the reggae music playing from speakers hanging in the trees. Jimmy Cliff. Toots and the Maytals. Bob Marley, too.

Lola's is named for a pig that long ago went on to her great reward; today the bar's mascot is the swine's rather large daughter, Lolita. I begin reciting a bit of Nabokov— *"light of my light, fire of my loin"*—in her honor, even though there was nothing nubile about this sow. Soon, wait staff are fetching rounds of mojitos, and my rather spartan chair feels as comfortable as a La-Z-Boy. I find myself mesmerized by the Pacific rhythmically swelling and breaking in front of me and the island music pulsating from the palms. The smile on my face only gets bigger as I feel the sand between my toes and let the drabs of sunlight cutting through the fronds gently warm my face. Then the food arrives. Cerviche made of freshly caught shrimp and mahi-mahi. Slices of raw tuna mixed with soy sauce and wasabi. And more rum.

I start gazing at a surfer catching a wave in the distance, and that gets me thinking about a cinematic factoid I had learned at dinner the night before: some of the beaches in this area served as locations for the epic surfer film *Endless Summer.*

That suddenly seems more than a little appropriate, for this is a visit I never want to end.

As surprising a golf destination as Costa Rica may be, its neighbor to the north, Nicaragua, may be an even more unlikely place to play the game. For one thing, only two

18-hole courses currently operate in Nicaragua, which is slightly larger than New York State and the largest country in Central America. It is also dirt poor, and the second most impoverished country in the Western Hemisphere. Very few *Nicas* can afford to tee it up, and little money has ever been devoted to the development of golf in a place where the most popular sports for locals are soccer and baseball—and where its prime tourism market consists of backpackers lured by ecotouring and the excellent opportunities to hike, bird, surf, and fish. Nor has there been much in the way of inducements created to lure players to this scenic land, which is bordered by the Pacific Ocean on the west and the Caribbean Sea to the east.

There is also the matter of politics. The Sandinista National Liberation Front, or FSLN, has ruled Nicaragua for most of the past three decades, and leaders of that left-wing movement no doubt view golf as little more than a corrupt pursuit of the uber-wealthy. Or at the very least, they should think that way if they want to stay true to their ideological roots. And how's that going to help grow the game?

But golf may actually be finding a place in this nation, thanks largely to an amenable and very successful local business magnate named Don Carlos Pellas and the opening this past winter of a stylish David McLay Kidd course by a secluded Pacific beach on which Pellas, who is regarded as the richest man in Nicaragua, used to camp as a boy. The par-72 track is the centerpiece of a sumptuous $250 million resort called Mukul that he has built here. The early returns on that impressive creation—and a Mike Young track at the Monte Cristo Beach and Golf Club that is being constructed by other developers some thirty miles up the coast—suggest that golf can certainly exist and maybe even prosper in a country now run by ex-guerillas. In fact, the sport may one day become a primary reason to visit.

I did not think such a thing was possible after I landed in Managua in late January, our plane banking over one of the country's seven active volcanoes on final approach, and began driving from Augusto C. Sandino International Airport, named after the celebrated Nicaraguan revolutionary, to Mukul, which is the Mayan word for "secret." It's not that the country or the people seem the least bit hostile, to golf or to international travelers. On the contrary, it feels immediately like a warm and welcoming place. It also makes me feel as if I have time traveled to the 1940s. Fields of sugar cane and bananas stretch out in all directions from the bumpy two-lane road down which we are motoring. Brahma cows lazily graze in scrubby pastures, and goats scurry around the rugged leas in small packs. Scrawny horses nibble on grass by the side of the blacktop, as locals lead ox-drawn carts down the road, delivering fruits and vegetables to vendors who run stands along the way. We race past small villages, made up mostly of wood shacks with corrugated tin roofs. And sometimes, the road just stops, as if the pavers suddenly ran out of asphalt. Then, it reappears, just as abruptly, a mile or two away.

But my sentiments about the possibility of golf here changes when I arrive at Mukul and see the resort for the first time.

The Pacific catches my eyes first, its cerulean waters fairly glistening in the midday sun. The waves produce long, crescent-shaped lines of white foam that dissipate as soon as they hit the pale beige sand of the beach. Small lines of pelicans glide over the tops of those breakers, searching for baitfish and occasionally diving into the surf.

Next, I notice the golf course. With his usual exuberance, Kidd tells me it represents his return to making golf courses like Bandon Dunes again, ones that are as fun as they are challenging, where there are plenty of places for the rec-

reational player to bail out and good opportunities to recover
from bad shots. He's been understandably stung by criticism
that some of his more recent efforts, at the Castle Course in
St. Andrews, Scotland, for example, and Tetherow in Bend,
Oregon, resulted in courses that are impossibly difficult—and
in some cases, even unfair.

Rather than pout, Kidd considerd a new way to go. His
course at Mukul, laid out along hills and flats overlooking
the ocean, is a reflection of that. Wide-open fairways and
elevated tees that make driving a gas. Slopes that a player
could use to run balls onto greens. Beguiling designs like
the par-three 15th, which he aptly describes as a combination Redan/Biarritz, and is the sort of hole that is so enticing and joyous that a player wants to hit more than one tee
shot, no matter how the first turned out. The par-five 16th
is an uphill tester that forces golfers to clear arroyos on the
way to a meaty green. The par-three finisher, with a green
that backs right up to the beach, is a visual stunner as well as
a damn hard par—even though it only measures 167 yards
from the tips. Your yardage had better be right, and your cal-
culations of the ever-present wind accurate, if you have any
hope of making a three.

The case for golf making a run in Nicaragua gets even
stronger as I stroll the property after my game. Mukul has
thirty-eight individual, very private, and exceptionally well-
appointed villas. Each boasts a private pool as well as butler service, an outdoor shower, and bathrooms the size of
squash courts. There is also a spa on the property, and it
comprises six individually themed *casitas* on a hill overlooking the beach. One is modeled after a Turkish sweat bath,
but I opt for the dwelling dubbed Rainforest and enjoy a
most relaxing bit of hydrotherapy.

The Nicaraguan entrepreneur who built Mukul, Don
Carlos Pellas, has a number of substantial business interests,

among them rum. His offerings under the Flor de Cana brand provide another way to kick back here. I especially appreciate an eighteen-year-old rum called Centenario, which I first tried in a tasting room that Pellas built off the open-air lobby at Mukul. Splash a little soda water into a glass of that caramel-colored elixir along with a few cubes of ice, squeeze a bit of lime on top, and you are in cocktail heaven. In addition, Pellas set up a spacious humidor featuring the top Cuban brands as well as several of Nicaragua's best, including my favorite, the Flor de las Antillas, which *Cigar Aficionado* named Cigar of the Year in 2012. I find myself visiting both *salas* at the end of each of my days there.

On my last afternoon at Mukul, I head back to my villa after another 18 holes of golf to enjoy a final rum and cigar on the terrace by my pool. The sun has just set, and the horizon is a glowing band of red-orange. I gaze at it for a moment and reconsider the assessments I had made earlier in the day.

Done this way, golf most definitely has a place here. It might even induce the Sandinistas to play.

25

BERMUDA AND THE CARIBBEAN
Paradise Found

ISLANDS ARE AN ALLURE FOR MANY REASONS. THEIR azure waters, for starters, along with sweeping views of seemingly endless seas. The soothing breezes that blow day and night, gently rattling palms and tousling hair, and the sun that beats down upon their beaches with comforting warmth. The fresh seafood they offer diners is always an attraction, and so are the potent rums that are made from their sugar cane. The best islands have a way of not only calling people to them but also inducing a desire among its denizens to live the sort of carefree life that Jimmy Buffet and his Parrotheads promote. Booze in the blender and shrimp beginning to boil, indeed. It all sounds and feels so good.

Then, there is the golf, and some of the best in the world can be found on such islands. Bermuda and Barbados, to name but two. The Dominican Republic, too. My advice is to drink a margarita or two and come on down.

Consider Bermuda. It may be a small nation, a fishhook-shaped collection of islands only twenty-one square miles in size with a population of just seventy thousand people. But it is a true superpower when it comes to golf. That's because Bermuda has more layouts (seven) per capita than any place on earth and year-round weather that is perfectly suited for the royal and ancient game, with temperatures rarely falling below 60 degrees. Even in winter. And the courses there combine great design with first-rate conditioning, ever-present winds, and jaw-dropping vistas.

The jewel in Bermuda's golfing crown is the Mid Ocean Club outside Tucker's Town, which was once a small farming and fishing burg but is now a second-home community whose residents include former New York City mayor Michael Bloomberg and Ross Perot. Designed by the great Charles Blair Macdonald and constructed by his protégé Seth Raynor, Mid Ocean is a 6,548-yard masterpiece with stylish renditions of the great golf holes of Europe and the British Isles. Like the par-three 3rd, an awesome Eden with the green perched on cliffs overlooking the Atlantic. And the 13th, which may be the best version of a Biarritz Macdonald and Raynor ever created. It requires a 240-yard tee shot to clear the characteristic swale and get to the middle of the massive, well-bunkered green. And then you have to putt.

Mid Ocean opened for play in 1924, and the story of its founding is as delicious as its routing. It begins with one of the owners of a local steamship company looking at golf as a way to develop Bermuda and asking Macdonald to accompany him on a trip there to see about building a course. Macdonald was keen for an overseas job at the time, in large part because he and his golfing friends needed another place they could tee it up—and drink after their rounds. Prohibition, you see, had just taken hold in the States, all but closing down their favorite 19th holes. In time, the developers found suitable land for the

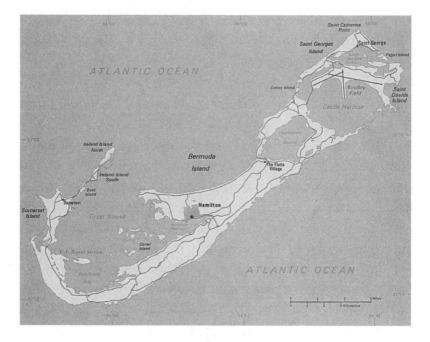

course, and Macdonald and Raynor drew up plans, needing two years to complete construction.

Mid Ocean quickly became a favorite among discerning golfers and has attracted its share of luminaries over the years, including Dwight Eisenhower, the Duke of Windsor, and Babe Ruth. Ruth famously hit eleven golf balls into the water one day trying to drive the par-four 5th hole. Winston Churchill also visited Mid Ocean, but not being a golfer he never made it onto the course. He did, however, quench his thirst at the clubhouse bar on a couple of occasions.

Next to Mid Ocean is another wonderful track at the Tucker's Point Golf Club. Originally laid out in 1932 by another Macdonald disciple, Charles Bank, it was deftly revamped a decade ago by Roger Rulewich, once the lead designer for the Robert Trent Jones team. This course features some fabulous downhill tee shots from coral rock outcroppings that are fun to play no matter where your drive ends up. Roosters and chickens scratch for food along the edges of the fairways, while colorful stands of oleander and hibiscus rustle in the breeze. The setting is so enchanting that when I admire the stretches of ocean and clusters of traditional Bermuda homes laid out before me, their stepped roofs painted white and walls soft pastels, it feels as if I am hitting into a Winslow Homer painting.

It is only a thirty-minute cab ride from Tucker's Point to another Bermudian golfing gem, Riddell's Bay, which is located in Warwick Parish in the southwest. The par-70 layout designed by Devereux Emmet is tight, tidy, and scenic, like the island territory itself, measuring a mere 5,854 yards from the back tees.

Riddell's Bay is the oldest course in Bermuda, having opened in 1922. It winds around a small peninsula that juts into Little Sound, and I smile as I step to the second tee and gaze at the ruins on a nearby island of the territory's first airport, where seaplanes used to land. Driver is usually best left in the bag here. But the greens on a couple of short par-fours are reachable, which means I cannot resist pulling out the Big Dog when I play them. Even if that move often leads to trouble. Water vistas are also a hallmark of the course, especially from the tee of the par-four 8th, which doglegs to the right and forces golfers to hit some portion of their tee shots over the water, the majestic Gibbs Hill lighthouse looming in the distance.

A little farther down the South Road is Port Royal, which opened in 1970 and was recently restored by Rulewich. Owned by the Bermudian government, it boasts several seaside holes that would fit in nicely at Cypress Point, especially the par-three 16th, which hugs the water. The par-71 course also has a bit of heft to it, playing more than 6,800 yards from the back tees and is so well regarded that it has been a frequent host of the PGA Grand Slam of Golf, a silly season event that features the winner of that year's major championships.

To be fair, the quality of Bermuda golf falls off somewhat after that foursome. But no player would ever tire of teeing it up on those four tracks. Nor would he, or she, lack for things to do off the golf course while visiting there.

Settled in 1609 by shipwrecked English colonists bound for Jamestown, Virginia, Bermuda is an overseas territory that exudes a decidedly British feel. Queen Elizabeth II is still considered the official head of state, and businessmen wear shorts and knee socks to their offices. Members of Parliament don white wigs whenever they enter the Senate or House of Assembly, and afternoon tea is served throughout the land each day at four o'clock. Yet Bermuda also boasts strong social and cultural influences from other parts of the world, primarily Africa, the Caribbean, and Portugal, giving it an overall ethos as beguiling as it is diverse.

Many of Bermuda's beaches are iridescent pink, thanks to the bits of sea invertebrates like coral, clams, and sea snails that have been crushed and ground by waves that constantly beat against its shores. I can never stop gawking at the vast waters surrounding it, some swathes aquamarine in color and others deep blue, brownish clusters of reefs visible just below the surface, the jagged rocks teeming with fish of all shapes, sizes, and colors. I find it very easy to loll on the stretches of sand there, reading and napping, and to swim and snorkel in the ocean. Nor do I have any trouble enjoying my favorite rum there, an ebon elixir called Gosling's Black Seal. It tastes awfully good on the rocks with a squeeze of lime and also mixes brilliantly with ginger beer to make the essential island drink—a Dark & Stormy.

A drink, by the way, that is nearly as good as the golf.

I have a tendency to get contemplative when I dip into the rum, and one of my most recent revelations is that when it comes to golf, I am pretty much a water guy. I prefer my courses on oceans, inlets, and estuaries, and I will travel far and wide to play them. I enjoy gazing across rugged seas whenever I tee it up and love listening to the surf crash into rocky cliffs during rounds. I even relish the winds that are ever present on coastal courses and I like hitting golf shots over stretches of water.

In many ways, I believe the game is best enjoyed in places like those, which is why I love Bermuda as a golf destination. It is also the reason I have so much fun playing in the Dominican Republic, for the easternmost tip of this land has as many good golf holes on the water as any on earth. And I mean right on the water, so close that even the slightest mishit goes into the drink. It also helps that this Caribbean country on which Christopher Columbus landed in 1492 boasts some of the most temperate weather anywhere, as well as a wealth of first-rate track designs.

I think of all that when I play the Corales and La Cana courses at the Punta Cana resort, laid out by Tom Fazio and P. B. Dye, respectively, and realize that five of the holes at Corales hug the Atlantic Ocean as do four at La Cana. The following morning, I venture to the nearby Cap Cana resort to tee it at Punta Espada, and happily discover that the Jack Nicklaus track there has a total of nine holes on the water, all postcard scenic and full of pleasure. And then I find myself on Pete Dye's famous Teeth of the Dog course at Casa de Campo, with seven golf holes running along the rugged, coral coast of the Caribbean, the waves sometimes breaking so hard that seawater leaps into the air mere feet from where I am teeing my Titleists or lining up putts.

By my count, that's twenty-five water holes on four courses, and if you want some perspective of what an embarrassment of aquatic riches that is, consider that water only comes into play on four holes at hallowed Cypress Point. Or that Punta Espada has as many golf holes on the Atlantic as Pebble Beach does on the Pacific. And even when you are not hard on the sea on these Dominican courses, chances are you can still see and appreciate the water. Most of the holes at Corales and La Cana have views of the Atlantic, for example, as do those at Punta Espada. The same goes for Teeth of the Dog, and even the Dye Fore course at Casa de Campo gives you a plethora of sea vistas on the first nine as well as seven holes on the second one that loom over the Chavon River as it cuts through a canyon three hundred feet below. Then there is the matter that many holes on these tracks also play over and around lakes and ponds.

Water is never out of sight or mind in the DR. Which is reason enough in my mind to visit again and again.

The most celebrated of the Dominican's seaside courses is also the oldest of the bunch, Teeth of the Dog. Pete Dye laid out that track in an area once known for the sugar cane that grew there—and the sugar mill that operated in the town of La Romana. It became the centerpiece of Casa de Campo, which is now a high-end resort with a sumptuous hotel, a community of well-appointed villas, a spacious marina, and 81 holes of golf. Named for the way local workers described how the rock coral resembled *diente del perro,* or Teeth of the Dog, during construction, it was quickly heralded as among the best courses the Hall of Fame architect ever built and dubbed the finest layout in the Caribbean. Not many golfers argued with those assertions. Especially after they played the four water holes on the front, and then 15, 16, and 17 on the way in. Bordered by the sea and frequently buffeted by trade winds, these holes make golfers feel as if they are hitting shots from lookout points into natural panoramas so gorgeous they belong on the cover of *National Geographic*—especially the three par-threes, strategic *hoyos* that require mid or long irons to reach greens guarded by sand and sea. The seaside views of the inland holes are also worth savoring, as are the colorful sweeps of bougainvillea and hibiscus growing throughout the property and the towering groves of coconut palms swaying gently in the wind.

The DR is a place of terrific character, on and off the course. In local villages, for example, meringue music blares out of boom boxes as Dominicans chat excitedly outside bars and butcher shops, fish stores and cafeterias. Some folks sell pineapples and plantains from makeshift stands, while others lead donkey carts laden with root vegetables as workers cut sugar cane in the fields. On dirt fields, kids play baseball, chattering with each other as they scoop up grounders and snag line drives, and dream of making it to the Major Leagues in the States. Like so many of their countrymen. Needless to say, trips to town can be as much fun as the golf itself.

A chance to play Teeth is alone worth the trip. But there are other quality golf courses. Such as the Links at Casa de Campo, and the course at La Romana Country Club. Dye designed both of those tracks, and while they do not have the sorts of dramatic water holes that make Teeth so celebrated, they nonetheless boast strong designs as well as some pretty good views of the Caribbean. His son P. B. built La Cana in 2001 at the Punta Cana resort, which features a modestly priced, family-oriented beachfront hotel as well as a much higher-end boutique inn, Tortuga Bay, with each of its thirty rooms designed by Dominican native and longtime resort resident Oscar de la Renta. The addition of La Cana, which not only included four holes right on the Atlantic but another ten with clear ocean views, gave golfers another first-rate place to tee it up in the DR when it came online. So did the addition of a new P. B. Dye track at Punta Cana, dubbed Hacienda. The Dye Fore course that Pete constructed at Casa de Campo in 2003 is an additional draw. Again, this is not a water track per se, but the Marina nine that opened the layout played right down to the sea, the Caribbean serving as a deep blue backdrop to most tee shots and approaches. And while players have to head inland for the back nine, called Chavron, it winds spectacularly on property some three hundred feet above the river gorge of that same name, with several greens and tees perched picturesquely on cliffs.

What really put the Dominican in rarified golfing air was the opening of Punta Espada in Cap Cana in 2006 and then Corales at Punta Cana, with the Cape-style 18th hole there wrapping itself around the rocky shore of Corales Bay. Taken together, those tracks give traveling golfers fourteen more of those seaside beauties to enjoy. Fourteen more opportunities to gawk at golf holes along the coast. Fourteen more ways to lose their golf balls. And fourteen more reasons to make their way to the Dominican. Where so much good golf is played on the water.

Golf is also a very good reason to visit Barbados, another favorite Caribbean isle. To be sure, the island nation is known in the broader travel world for being the place where Mount Gay rum is made. And when visitors are not swilling that luscious nectar to the soulful beat of ska music in Bajan rum shacks, they are sipping it on the country's sugar-sand beaches.

But there are other attributes of this former British colony, which was settled in 1625 and lies only 270 miles northeast of Venezuela. Surfing and sailing, for example. Snorkeling and deep-sea fishing, too. History buffs can enjoy tours of one of the oldest synagogues in the Western Hemisphere (built in 1654) and also the only house outside the United States George Washington ever lived in. Then, there's the dining, as food is taken as seriously in Barbados as rum. In fact, the roster of eateries is so impressive that Tim and Nina Zagat published their first dining guide in the Caribbean there in 2006.

But what about golf? At the end of the twentieth century, there was only one course of note in Barbados, an enjoyable 18-hole track called Royal Westmoreland that Robert Trent

Jones Jr. laid out in 1994. However, developers have opened three superb layouts there since the turn of the century, all in the west coast parish of St. James. And that's moved the royal and ancient game much higher up of the list of rationales for arranging a visit.

My first taste of golf in Barbados came in the fall of 2006 with a round at Royal Westmoreland, where one-time Masters winner Ian Woosnam has a home. On that same trip, I played the Tom Fazio–designed Country Club course at the nearby Sandy Lane resort, which is where Tiger Woods and Elin Nordegren married in much happier times, and I must confess to being instantly smitten not only with the layout of both courses but also the scenic land on which they are routed.

Royal Westmoreland winds through coral canyons and over grassy hills offering sweeping views of the Caribbean and lots of downhill tee shots over gaping ravines. Sandy Lane proved to be just as enticing with its swathes of bougainvillea, the red- and magenta-colored flowers bursting from the dull green scrubs like stars from a clear, dark sky. I also marveled at the famed green monkeys scampering around the groves of almond and mahogany trees, and at the stories I heard of how the primates first arrived on Barbados with seventeenth-century traders from West Africa.

Unfortunately, I never got to play the other 18-hole layout at Sandy Lane, a second Fazio design named after those monkeys (whose fur is not really green but sometimes gives off a hue of that color). That's because only guests at the ultra-high-priced resort may tee it up there, and I was staying elsewhere. But I did drive a golf cart around the Green Monkey and fell hard for the way Fazio deftly worked it in and around a coral rock quarry, making some holes feel as if you were playing in an amphitheater. Tee times on that track run for only an hour each day, and it handles no more than a thousand rounds a year.

A few years later, I returned to Barbados to play at the newest—and I believe best—course on the island. Called Apes Hill, it is the result of collaboration between Bajan industrialist Sir Charles Williams, who runs one of the largest construction companies in the Caribbean, and Jerry Barton's Landmark Land Co., which has built a number of superlative golf courses and communities over the years, among them La Quinta and Kiawah Island.

The lush layout at Apes Hill is the centerpiece of a lavish golf and polo community. The course cuts across hills that rise as high as a thousand feet above sea level and features rolling meadows, dense tropical forests, and coral rock outcroppings, with the Atlantic and Caribbean serving as distant backdrops.

Good as those visuals are, however, the design at Apes Hill is even better, as it takes advantage of the diverse terrain to present a wide range of shot-making possibilities and bestows the track a linksy feel by allowing golfers to run shots onto the greens. A premium is put on playing the angles, too, rewarding those golfers who hit their drives to the proper side of fairways with much easier approaches. I like the mix of long and short par-fours that force me, literally, to use every club in my bag and come away thinking that Apes Hill has as good a collection of par-threes as I've ever found on one course, with testy greens of varying lengths tucked in front of coral walls, along streams, beside grass-faced bunkers, and next to dense swathes of jungle.

The Mount Gay is good here, to be sure. But golf is now a pretty strong reason to go as well. To Barbados, and also to those other isles.

26

COLOMBIA
Birdies and Bogota

I HAD A VERY VISCERAL REACTION WHEN MY AIRLINER landed at El Dorado International Airport. And I expressed more than a modicum of anxiety as I suddenly appreciated where I had just landed.

What the hell am I doing here?

The question arose mostly over concern as to how safe I would be in this bounteous, South American land, rich in natural beauty and resources and blessed with a populace as hospitable as it is hardworking. But Colombia has also been wracked with wars and insurrections ever since Simón Bolívar liberated it from the colonial clutches of Spain in the early 1800s. One particularly difficult time, at the turn of the twentieth century, came to be known as the Thousand Day War. Another era, beginning in 1948 and lasting a couple of decades, was dubbed *La Violencia.* Then came the troubles born of the murderous cocaine trade in the 1980s and 1990s, as well as a de facto civil war with leftist rebels. During those times, Colombia was the sort of place travelers avoided at all costs. Which is why I was having deep doubts about my judgment.

What *was* I doing here?

I wondered more about that as I drove to my hotel in Bogota, a city as crowded (roughly ten million residents) as it is high in elevation (8,600 feet). Of course, I knew things had gotten better in recent years, thanks to a succession of leaders committed to taking on the *narcoistas* and guerillas and a remarkable ability among its citizenry to deal with adversity. I also realized the major cocaine cartels had been crushed and the guerilla group known as FARC more or less defeated. I was aware that these days, traffic was a much bigger concern in this city—often described as the Athens of South America for its many museums and libraries—than bombings or kidnappings.

Still, I wasn't entirely comfortable about where I had actually taken myself when I went to sleep that first night in Bogota.

I felt the same way when I walked into a mostly deserted hotel lobby early the next morning to get a cup of coffee. But those sentiments quickly changed when former US president Bill Clinton strode through the front door. Alone. There was no security around him, and he walked right over, his right hand extended and his eyes meeting my surprised gaze.

"How are you doing?" he asked in his raspy, Arkansas drawl. "I've been flying all night from Africa."

"Good to meet you, Mr. President," I uttered as I grasped his hand. Still stunned by his sudden appearance and thinking of nothing else to say, I simply inquired: "What brings you to Colombia?"

He smiled warmly as he eyed the golf bag I had stood up earlier by the coffee urn. "The same thing that seems to have brought you here," he replied. "The golf."

I soon learned that Clinton wasn't kidding. Several years before, he and philanthropist Frank Guistra had established the Clinton Guistra Sustainable Growth Initiative (CGSGI) in Colombia to develop sustainable, market-driven businesses; strengthen child nutrition; and expand access to health services. And the CGSGI was one of the charitable organizations benefiting from the season-opening event of what is now the Web.com Tour, the Pacific Rubiales Colombia Championship. The former president had made the trip so he could promote the good work of his initiative—and play in the Pro-Am.

That tournament was also what had led me and my trepidations to Colombia, notebooks and golf clubs in tow. My chance encounter with Clinton reassured me that this was a much safer place to visit than it used to be. Especially after a member of his security detail later told me there was no way the former president would have come to Bogota a decade ago given the threats of violence that existed then.

At the same time, I considered Clinton's passion for the royal and ancient game—and the fact that he had brought his clubs along. That, and the presence of a tour event, told me that there must be some pretty good golf in Colombia.

I soon learned that Colombia is indeed a fine place to tee it up. The country boasts more than fifty courses, and some feature the design work of Jack Nicklaus, Gary Player, Robert Trent Jones, and Ron Garl. One of the most celebrated of the eighteen tracks in and around the nation's capital is the Country Club of Bogota, a leafy retreat on which the Web.com tourney is played each year. Founded in 1917, it is the oldest club in the country, a parklands track near the center of town with verdant fairways and greens lined by towering eucalyptus trees. The Bogota area is home to other compelling layouts, among them the San Andres Golf Club, La Pradera de Potosi, and Club el Rincon. La Cima, too, where the elevation at the clubhouse tops nine thousand feet and clouds often linger in the valleys *below* the fairways and greens. It's the second highest golf course in Latin America, and my caddie aptly described the hike up the fairway to the 5th green as a "stairway to heaven." Even a poorly hit drive seems to fly forever in the thin air here.

There are a number of solid tracks in other parts of Colombia, which is the third largest country in South America (after Brazil and Argentina) and has a population of forty-six million. Golf Club Manizales and Club Campestre Pereira are located in the rugged, coffee-producing hills west of Bogota. Club Campestre Medellin is set in the mountainous metropolis where the notorious drug lord Pablo Escobar once reigned—and where multiple PGA Tour winner Camilo Villegas learned to play the game. None of those tracks are reason alone to venture to this land for the golf, but they are fun courses, well conditioned and well designed. They not only give visitors a chance to tee it up but also offer an opportunity to get a feel for the scenic splendor of the Colombian countryside. And it is quite a countryside, for Colombia is one of the more ecologically diverse countries on the planet, with sweeping Caribbean beaches to the northeast and the thick, Amazon jungle in the south as well as high savannah plains and the Andes Mountains.

I enjoyed every chance I had to tour this territory. On or off the golf course. A two-day trek to the Pereira and Manizales area showed me a more agricultural aspect of Colombia, with patches of small family farms dotting the hills. Some were filled with rows of plantain trees and others with coffee plants, and I learned to tell the ages of those crops by the shade of the green of their leaves. In time, I could also identify many of the bird species that flourished there, and one morning before golf I counted more than sixty-five. I figured that is a pretty good number until my host, Carolina

Mejia, told me that Colombia boasts more than nineteen hundred avian species.

I spent a weekend on the coffee farm that Carolina's family has run in these hills about 110 miles west of Bogota for several generations, staying in their *paisa* and sleeping some nights in a hammock hanging on the porch. I started each day there with a cup or two of coffee brewed from beans harvested from their plantation, watching the sun cast its first light across the plots of coffee plants, with their clusters of reddish fruit growing on the hillsides, and the occasional plantain grove, where the trees have leaves as big as surfboards. After that morning repose, I took walks across the property with Carolina and her mother, Maria. Maria always carried a walking stick in one hand and a *peinilla*, which is a sort of machete, in the other. I savored the scent of jasmine that often filled the air and noticed plots of tomatoes and groves of avocado and guava trees, too. And birds. Hundreds of birds. In the afternoons, I played golf. My favorite course, at the Club Campestre Pereira, was about an hour's drive away up and down steep and narrow roads, and it is a delightful, youngish track that offers a wide range of shot options and angles. The place has a tropical feel to it, and that sensation is only heightened as the sun climbs higher in the sky, and both the temperature and humidity rise with it. Iguanas scurry across the fairways on some holes, and I chuckled when my playing partner once told me to "aim at the mango tree" as I stood on the tee of one par-four. It was not exactly the sort of line I hear during my regular games back home in Connecticut.

After my weekend in the countryside I returned to Bogota, and although traffic-choked and chaotic, the city nonetheless has plenty of charm. Especially in the hilly enclave known as La Candelaria, with its colonial-style architecture, cobblestoned streets, and eclectic collection of bars and art galleries. This is where the elegant Teatro de Cristobal Colon opera house is located, as well as the Plaza de Bolívar, site of the Colombian Congress and the Palace of Justice and the place where dancers, musicians, and vendors gather daily to entertain and entice visitors. Bolívar lived in this part of town, and the Botero Museum is situated there today, with its compelling collection by Colombia's noteworthy figurative artist Fernando Botero.

Candeleria is also home to La Puerta Falsa (which translates into "the False Door"). A cramped, two-story eatery that opened around the time Bolívar liberated Colombia, it often served breakfast to the celebrated revolutionary. I marveled at the history of the spot as I settled into a chair, enjoying its excellent hot chocolate and sumptuous tamales wrapped in banana leaves.

I found many other places of interest in and around Bogota. Like the Museo del Oro, which documents the role gold has played in Colombia's history. The Salt Cathedral in Zipaquira, where miners built a vast chapel more than six hundred feet below ground that attracts as many as three thousand worshippers for Sunday services, is a must-visit, even for those pilgrims who get a little queasy when they find themselves so far underground. Another must is the cable car ride up to the charming church at Montserrate, which provides a sweeping panorama of the city that takes away whatever breath a visitor may still have at that height (more than 10,300 feet). Dinner at the San Isidro restaurant next door is a triumph, too, for the superb food and service and also the excellent setting and view. I especially liked the fireplace by my table the night I dined there, for the atmosphere it provided as well as the warmth, as temperatures outside fell into the 40s during our meal, and I could feel the high altitude chill.

Riding the tram down from San Isidro that night, I could not help but think of another conversation I had with President Clinton this trip, as we both warmed up on the range at the Country Club of Bogota before our respective tee times in the Pro-Am. He told me this was his third visit to Colombia since he had become an ex-president. And he vowed to come back soon.

My hope is that I am able to do the same.

THE LISTS

FOR MOST GOLFERS, SPENDING TIME TOGETHER AFTER their rounds is as good as the games they have just played. For the drinks they share with each other in wood-paneled pubs and cozy grill rooms and for the stories they tell of heroic shots hit and bets won. Those moments often induce much broader discussions about golf itself, and a favorite exercise among many of my golfing mates is sharing opinions on the best things in the sport. The top courses in different parts of the world, perhaps. Or the most comfortable locker rooms. The finest places for lunch and the clubs with the headiest wine cellars. And, not surprisingly, the greatest 19th holes.

Over the years, I have participated in a number of those conversations, absorbing the thoughts of golfers for whom I have strong respect and developing some opinions of my own along the way. They are the inspiration for the following lists of Top Fives.

TOP FIVE GOLF COURSES

Old World

1. The Old Course (St. Andrews, Scotland)
2. The Championship Course—Royal Dornoch (Scotland)
3. The Ailsa Course—Turnberry (Scotland)
4. Dunluce Links—Royal Portrush (Northern Ireland)
5. Muirfield (Scotland)

Honorable Mention: Waterville Golf Links (Ireland)

Oftentimes, great golf courses are as much about their settings and histories as they are about their actual designs. Which is why the Old comes out on top here, and why the Ailsa and Muirfield also rank so high in my book. Dornoch combines those qualities with a sort of mystical ethos due to its quiet and quaint isolation that always make me feel as if I am playing in a dream. And there is nothing quite as spiritual in golf as the Mass Hole at Waterville, a par-three that plays into dunes where local Catholics once risked their lives by holding secret services.

New World

1. Cypress Point Club (Pebble Beach, California)
2. Augusta National Golf Club (Georgia)
3. Pine Valley Golf Club (New Jersey)
4. National Golf Links of America (Long Island)
5. Sand Hills Golf Club (Mullen, Nebraska)

Honorable Mentions: Country Club of Fairfield (Connecticut) and Chicago Golf Club (Wheaton, Illinois)

It is hard to distinguish much between the Big Three here—Cypress, Augusta, and Pine Valley. They could not be more different in terms of architecture and locale, and their heritages are rich and deep. But each course is brilliantly designed, and the total experiences there are as otherworldly as the golf itself, making any visit pure joy. It is much the same way with the National, which Charles Blair Macdonald founded as a way to introduce Americans to the traditional links game. As for Sand Hills, it is one of the modern wonders of the golf world, and the place that started the trend toward site-based golf development that happily led to the creation of retreats like Bandon Dunes and Cabot Links.

Outposts

1. West Course—Royal Melbourne Golf Club (Australia)
2. Lost Farm—Barnbougle (Tasmania)
3. Royal Dar Es Salaam Golf Club (Rabat, Morocco)
4. Mid Ocean Golf Club (Bermuda)
5. Kauri Cliffs (New Zealand)

Honorable Mentions: Teeth of the Dog—Casa de Campo (Dominican Republic) and Kingston Heath Golf Club (Australia)

Pity the player who is not able to sample the golfing riches that exist in the farthest flung places on the planet, for there are some wonderful courses there. Start with the Melbourne Sand Belt, which has several layouts on which the great Alister MacKenzie once worked, Royal Melbourne West and Kingston Heath among them. The two courses at Barnbougle have made the previously obscure Australian state of Tasmania a must-visit for peripatetic players, and they will also find a true golfing surprise at Royal Dar Es Salaam, which may be the best track Robert Trent Jones Sr. ever designed.

TOP FIVE 19TH HOLES

1. Men's Locker Room—Seminole Golf Club (North Palm Beach, Florida)
2. Terrace—Country Club of Fairfield (Connecticut)
3. Clubhouse and Terrace—Garden City Golf Club (Long Island)
4. Lawn behind the Clubhouse—Ekwanok Golf Club (Manchester, Vermont)
5. Bar—Dunvegan Hotel (St. Andrews, Scotland)

Honorable Mentions: Road Hole Bar—Old Course Hotel (St. Andrews) and Men's Locker Room—The Country Club (Brookline, Massachusetts)

No postround place in golf is quite like the Seminole locker room, with its high ceilings, spacious wood lockers, cozy easy chairs, and plaques honoring the winners of past club events—and featuring some of the biggest names in professional and amateur golf. Plus, the attendants mix some pretty good drinks from the bar there. The terrace at the Country Club of Fairfield offers sweeping views of Long Island Sound as well as the chance for members and their guests to watch golfers come up one of the best finishing holes in the American Northeast. Garden City is as congenial an after-golf retreat as exists in the game, whether you are lounging in its museum-like clubhouse or relaxing in one of the Adirondack chairs behind the green of the par-three 18th. And if there is a better and more convivial bar in the game than the one that Jack and Sheena Willoughby preside over at the Dunvegan Hotel in St. Andrews, I have yet to see it.

TOP FIVE GOLF LUNCHES

1. The Birdcage—National Golf Links of America (Long Island)
2. Prestwick Golf Club (Scotland)
3. River Wildlife (Kohler, Wisconsin)
4. Ben's Porch—Sand Hills Golf Club (Nebraska)
5. Stillwater Grill—Pebble Beach Golf Links (California)

Honorable Mentions: River Bar—The Cloister (Sea Island, Georgia) and Whisper Rock (Scottsdale, Arizona)

The Birdcage is an enclosed porch off the main clubhouse building at the National that feels like something of an aerie, with stunning views of the classic C. B. Macdonald course and the glimmering waters of Peconic Bay. Lunch at Prestwick, in coat and tie and with lots of whisky and wine, is exactly how the royal and ancient game should be enjoyed in its ancestral home. Ben's Porch at Sand Hills is spectacular in its simplicity, with bratwursts and burgers cooked to perfection on a small grill. And the shrimp at the River Bar in Sea Island, overlooking the very waters from which they are harvested, as a sweet as sherbet.

TOP FIVE HALFWAY HOUSES

1. The J Bar—Shinnecock Hills Golf Club (Long Island)
2. Diamante (Cabo San Lucas, Mexico)
3. Maidstone Club (Long Island)
4. Fisher's Island (New York)
5. Olympic Club (San Francisco)

Honorable Mention: Whistling Straits (Kohler, Wisconsin)

The margaritas at the turn at Diamante are sublime, as are the fish tacos. It is not unusual to want to linger at this spot overlooking the sand dunes at the very bottom of the Baja peninsula and beyond them the Pacific Ocean. Quirky is the best way to describe the tattered food truck that serves as a roving halfway house at Fisher's Island, but there is a certain hominess about it. And the peanut butter, jelly, and bacon sandwiches that are served are five-star good. As for golfers seeking midround refreshment at Shinnecock, they have the pleasure of entering the iconic Stanford White clubhouse and going right to the place known as the J Bar for food and drink.

TOP FIVE GOLF DESTINATIONS
FOR POSTROUND FUN

1. Marrakesh, Morocco—Tours of the Ancient Souk
2. Dublin, Ireland—Literary Pub Crawl
3. Laucala Island, Fiji—Deep-Sea Fishing
4. Cape Kidnappers, New Zealand—Kiwi Walks
5. Kohala Coast, Hawaii—Coffee Tasting

Honorable Mentions: Crans-sur-Sierre, Switzerland—Cow Fighting and Palestina, Colombia—Bird Watching

Although golf may be an impetus for travel, it is by no means the only reason to take to the road. I am always looking for fun things to do once my games are done. Getting to know Dublin's colorful pub culture by following in the footsteps of James Joyce and Brendan Behan, among other Irish literary giants, is a superlative way to unwind after 36 holes. So is joining a New Zealand naturalist in search of rare and endangered kiwis, or taking in a cow fight in the Swiss canton of Valais, where beefy bovines butt heads to determine who is the "queen."

TOP FIVE PRACTICE FACILITIES

1. Pine Valley (New Jersey)
2. Augusta National Golf Club (Georgia)
3. Merit Club (Chicago)
4. Frederica Golf Club (Sea Island, Georgia)
5. Diamante (Cabo San Lucas)

Honorable Mentions: Bandon Dunes (Oregon) and Whisper Rock (Arizona)

The double-ended ranges at Pine Valley, Bandon, and Whisper Rock make this very practice-averse player long to hit bucket after bucket of balls. The three practice holes at the Merit Club are what vault that facility onto this list, and I know that my handicap would drop a couple of strokes if I had regular access to the short-game areas at Frederica. But the gold standard is the Tournament Practice Facility at Augusta National, which is used only for the Masters and a couple of member events a year. To a man, the touring professionals will tell you there is nothing like it anywhere. As for Diamante, what's not to like about a range where music from artists as varied as Bruce Springsteen and Oscar Peterson is piped in?

TOP FIVE LOGOS

1. Fox Head—Myopia Hunt Club (South Hamilton, Massachusetts)
2. Milk Bottle—MacArthur Golf Club (Hobe Sound, Florida)
3. Caravel—Cabot Links (Cape Breton, Nova Scotia)
4. British and Scottish Flags—Frederica Golf Club (Georgia)
5. Scallop Shell—Kittansett Golf Club (Marion, Massachusetts)

Honorable Mentions: Lion's Head with Golf Ball in Mouth—Royal Dar Es Salaam Golf Club and Cow with Golf Club in Mouth—Stonewall Golf Club (Elverson, Pennsylvania)

Though I do not list any entries from the British Isles, I must confess to a certain weakness for the classic coat-of-arms style logo that many of those clubs possess, even though some of them are as big as beer coasters. Especially those that boast the word "Royal."

TOP FIVE GOLF TRIPS

1. St. Andrews (Scotland)
2. Melbourne Sand Belt (Australia)
3. Bandon Dunes (Oregon)
4. Dublin (Ireland)
5. South Africa (via Rovos Rail)

Honorable Mentions: Kohler (Wisconsin), Northwest Ireland, and Sea Island (Georgia)

While the South Africa golf safari on Rovos Rail is certainly the most unusual of these, it may actually be the most compelling. For the opportunity to travel across that staggeringly beautiful and varied land via vintage train coaches, where most cabins have queen beds and en suite bathrooms, and gourmet food and drink are served in a sumptuous dining car. As well as for the chance to enjoy afternoon game drives after your morning rounds of golf.

ACKNOWLEDGMENTS

Ever since I embarked on my first trip overseas, as a twelve-year-old lad visiting a very hip and happening London, England, in 1968, I have been trying to see the world and fill my passport with visa stamps. Among the many things I have learned through my adventures is that a proficient traveler must be an independent and self-sufficient soul. But he also has to channel Blanche DuBois on occasion and rely on the kindness of strangers—and friends. For guidance as to the most convivial places to eat, sleep, and drink as well as where to see the most interesting sights. And for direction when it comes to discerning the ethos of different locales and the characteristics that make them so entertaining and unique.

People have extended great kindness toward me over more than four decades of rather intensive touring. Their help has been particularly important over the past twenty years as my work as a golf writer has taken me from

Cape Town to Bogota, from Kona to Marrakesh, and from Turnberry to Tasmania. So has the support of those editors who have sent me on such wonderful journeys, to say nothing of the backing I have long received from my family whenever I have had to leave home for days, and sometimes weeks, at a time. All of which means I have many folks to thank—and much to thank them for.

First and foremost, I am greatly indebted to good friend Jim Nugent, who as my publisher at *Global Golf Post* has always given me the means to travel the world for what I believe is the best journal in sports—and then the space to recount those fabulous expeditions in its pages. In addition, he has quite generously allowed me to use significant portions of those travel features in this volume. My editors at the *Post*— Brian Hewitt, Mike Purkey, Lawrence Hollyfield, Mike Cullity, Tim Cronin, Jeff Barr, Sam Dolson, and Steve Ellis—handle my copy with great deftness and respect, and I appreciate the keen insight they offer as to the best ways to approach different subjects. Our design director, Barbara Ivins-Georgoudiou, boasts a brilliant eye as well as a terrific knack for making my stories look so good. She is also a delight to work with, as are colleagues Reese Wallace and Jamie Nugent, who so ably provide a wide range of logistical help.

While most of the travel writing I have done in recent years has been for the *Post*, I have occasionally taken to the road for other outlets. And I would be remiss if I did not proffer my heartfelt thanks to the editors of those fine journals, and the ways they, too, support and sustain my passion for travel writing. So here's to Andrew Powell, Duncan Christy, Gary Walther, and Phil Terzian—great guys and great wordsmiths all.

Over the years, I have used a number of travel operators to set up trips and sort out itineraries, and no one has been more helpful in that regard—or more fun and efficient to deal with—than Marty Carr of Carr Golf and Gordon and Colin Dalgleish of Perry Golf. I have also appreciated the ways that Bill Hogan of Wide World of Golf and the folks at Adventures in Golf have also served as very capable Sherpas when called upon.

Thanks also goes to the publisher of this tome, Rick Rinehart, for giving me the opportunity to write about a subject so near and dear to my heart. I am grateful for all he did to ensure that the final version of the book turned out so well.

Finally, I must pay tribute to my lovely wife, Cynthia, who warmly bids me "Adieu" each time I take to the road; cheerfully runs our household while I am gone as she also runs her own business, even in the face of hurricanes and blizzards; and seems genuinely happy to see me upon my return. And not once has she ever begrudged me all the golf I play during my trips—and the fine foods, wines, and spirits I am able to savor after my rounds. She is the best, as are our darling daughters Exa and Lydia, and I cherish our times at home as well as those occasions when we are able to hit the road together.

May there be many more of those in our future.

John Steinbreder
Redding, Connecticut

ABOUT THE AUTHOR

John Steinbreder is an award-winning journalist and the author of nineteen books (and currently working on his twentieth). A senior writer for *Global Golf Post*, he also contributes to Masters .com, the official Masters website. Previously, Steinbreder worked as a reporter for *Fortune* magazine, a writer/reporter for *Sports Illustrated*, and a senior writer for *Golfweek*. He has also produced articles for several prominent periodicals, including *The New York Times Magazine, Departures, Forbes Life, The Weekly Standard*, the *Wall Street Journal*, and *Time*. In addition, he composed chapters for a number of books, among them *The Sports Illustrated Almanac, 1001 Golf Holes to Play before You Die, A Walk in the Park*, and *The Final Four of Everything*. An avid golfer who carries a USGA index of six, Steinbreder has reported on the game on five continents, receiving ten honors for his work from the Golf Writers Association of America and seventeen from the International Network of Golf.